W9-CDT-254

pure
Vegetarian

pure Vegetarian

108

Indian-Inspired Recipes

to Nourish Body and Soul

LAKSHMI WENNAKOSKI-BIELICKI

Roost Books

BOSTON LONDON

2015

Roost Books
An imprint of Shambhala Publications, Inc.
Horticultural Hall
300 Massachusetts Avenue
Boston, Massachusetts 02115
roostbooks.com

© 2015 by Minna Wennakoski-Bielicki
All rights reserved. No part of this book may
be reproduced in any form or by any means,
electronic or mechanical, including photo-
copying, recording, or by any information
storage and retrieval system, without permission
in writing from the publisher.
9 8 7 6 5 4 3 2 1

Published in agreement with Stilton Literary
Agency, Finland.

First Edition
Printed in the United States of America

♾ This edition is printed on acid-free paper that
meets the American National Standards Institute
z39.48 Standard.
♻ Shambhala Publications makes every effort
to print on recycled paper. For more information
please visit www.shambhala.com.

Distributed in the United States by Penguin
Random House LLC and in Canada by Random
House of Canada Ltd

BOOK DESIGN BY SHUBHANI SARKAR

Library of Congress
Cataloging-in-Publication Data

Wennakoski-Bielicki, Lakshmi.
Pure vegetarian: 108 Indian-inspired recipes to
nourish body and soul / Lakshmi Wennakoski-
Bielicki.
    pages   cm.
Includes index.
ISBN 978-1-61180-144-6 (alk. paper)
1. Vegetarian cooking. I. Title.
TX837.W443 2015
641.5'636—dc23
2014019629

DEDICATED TO MY BELOVED GURUDEVA

nama om visnu-padaya krsna-presthaya bhu-tale
srimate suhotra svamin iti namine
namaste guru-hamsaya kali-prabhava-harine
prabhupada-siksa-vidyadbhuta pravacanena vai

CONTENTS

AUTHOR'S NOTE / ix

INTRODUCTION / 1

Part One
RECIPES

ABOUT THE RECIPES / 15

HOMEMADE DAIRY / 21

SPICES / 49

RICE, GRAINS & DAL / 63

VEGETABLE DISHES / 87

BREADS, SNACKS & SAVORIES / 129

SALADS, SEEDLINGS & SPROUTS / 159

CHUTNEYS, RAITAS & SAUCES / 179

DESSERTS / 199

DRINKS / 243

Part Two
MY INGREDIENTS
& KITCHEN TOOLS

INGREDIENTS / 257

KITCHENWARE / 287

GLOSSARY / 291

RESOURCES / 295

INDEX / 299

ABOUT THE AUTHOR / 307

AUTHOR'S NOTE

It is always exciting to meet someone new. You stretch to find a common ground on which to communicate and interact comfortably, and you respond to the other person's perspective and needs, whether or not you agree or disagree, simply because you are thrilled by his or her charisma and unique attributes. You rejoice at discovering what views you share and celebrate even those that are different because, like spices, these differences elevate an ordinary experience into something special.

That's how I anticipated it would be to write this book. I imagined you and I would be like two passengers in a cozy railroad car, immersed in a lively exchange about what cooking and food mean to both of us while sharing our traveling snacks.

Unfortunately, the train had hardly departed when I realized I was sitting alone and having a monologue. When you didn't join me at the first station, or the next, or any other one during the two years it took to write this book, I struggled to make sense of the landscape through which the train lurched and the purpose of my journey. I had gotten what seemed like a free ticket from the publisher and, like anyone wet behind the ears, I had grabbed it without weighing whether or not I was ready. Although doubts about my cooking skills raced through the mind while I was developing and testing the recipes, it was the nonrecipe content that produced real anxiety.

Again and again, I wondered if I knew your language. I don't mean just English but the private symbols you verbalize the world with. Would I be able to connect with you and contribute something genuine to your life? After all, I had taken up this journey in order to offer you a piece of the treasure I carry within my heart, sincerely believing it would make you happy. I battled with myself to find the best way to present it, and felt that each correction and revision of my book increased the distance between me and the station where you would join me. Why was it so difficult to speak about personal topics in such specific terms as recipes and cooking? No matter how much I groomed the words, they only scratched the surface of what I wanted to say. I worried that when you finally step onboard as a reader and take a seat opposite me, you won't find but a trail of crumbs.

Despite the trials I stumbled upon, there were also wonderful perks. The humming of the train created a steady rhythm that was fun and safe to follow. It made me reorganize my priorities and deepened my study, contemplation, and application of Vedic instructions.

And finally, we are here together, sharing a train car.

I am especially thankful for His Holiness Bhaktividya Purna Swami, who has influenced my spiritual growth more than anyone for the past several years by educating me about the knowledge, process, and goal of devotional service, *bhakti*. He has helped me to see directly and indirectly how everything is connected to the Absolute Truth.

Without the interest and energy of Rochelle Bourgault, my editor, you would not be holding this book in your hands. She had a vision, and she kindly pitched for me.

Tiina Kristoffersson, my literary agent, took care of the book contract and relentlessly explained the legal language. *Kiitos!*

My husband, Purnaprajna Prabhu, kept me on the pulse of the soul whenever he wasn't washing the dishes, taking out the garbage, and assisting with the photo shoots. His ability to see goodness and potential where there seems to be none and his steadfast encouragement made me write this book from the point of view of relationships.

I would like to credit my well-wishing friend Syama Radhika for asking, when she heard I was writing a cookbook, "What can you offer to a reader that no other author has published yet?" I kept looking for an answer to her question throughout the process, and I hope she will be satisfied to read my response.

Photographing the images was a challenge I needed assistance with. Thankfully, my friends Jaana Cowasji, Radha Vijaya, Madhuri Prema, and Keshava Madhava Prabhu rescued me at a crucial moment, with my sister-in-law, Nina, and beautiful goddaughter Charlotta.

pure
Vegetarian

INTRODUCTION

Like all cookbooks, *Pure Vegetarian* is a recipe collection that shares various cooking methods, techniques, and facts to advance your culinary skills. Colorful photographs cater a visual fare, engage your appetite, and get your creative juices flowing. Throughout the pages of recipes—from simple cheeses to spices, rice dishes, legumes, vegetables, snacks, salads, chutneys, desserts, and beverages—the instructions are simple and clear. If you are unfamiliar with any of the ingredients or foreign terms, you can refer to the glossary at the end of the book. I have also itemized my kitchenware to give you an idea of which utensils and appliances are practical to have on hand, and included a conversion table to help you change any volume, weight, or temperature into your standard unit. However, this is as far as the similarities between *Pure Vegetarian* and other cookbooks go.

By introducing the concept of yoga cuisine, I veer away from the culinary trends that fixate on taste buds, kitchen craft, or diet tips and encourage you to look beyond the physical, the moral, and even the social implications of eating. Food is a medium for relationships: milk, butter, flour, apples, sugar, and salt are but the means to experiences.

I often joke that an expert cook is also a matchmaker: to bring out the best in an eggplant, a dollop of ghee, and a handful of spices, you have to understand their characteristics and behavior as well as if you were assembling an orchestra or a basketball team. The more knowledge you have about their personalities—their temperament, strengths, interactions with others, and individual needs—the easier it will be to create a meal. But you also have to understand your role and must be inspired to wrap an apron around your waist in the first place. The way you see yourself in the world makes you sensitive to others' natures and needs, too.

Everyone craves fulfillment. You may be chasing after that tantalizing scent, taste, color, shape, or texture that magically transforms a sack of potatoes into a gourmet dish. Or you may find happiness in making a bowl of warm soup from organic produce and serving it at a homeless shelter. Or you may prefer spending a long afternoon at the table with those you love and care about, relishing the best of humanity. The motivation—why you are cooking—arises from your thoughts, desires, and values and affects the nature of your experience as a cook. You perceive the entire process of shopping, peeling, cutting, boiling, plating, sharing, and enjoying food through your own reality.

Linking consciousness and cooking is not a new discipline. The saints and sages of Vedic India, dating back thousands of years, were gastronomists who connected the physical, chemical, and biochemical nature of nourishment with spirituality and associated the laws of regulating digestion with the reciprocal dynamics among material energy, living beings, and transcendence. For them, "life" went far beyond the body and its psychological and intellectual faculties; it included the immortality of the soul. Our attitudes and actions align with (and contribute to) universal harmony. Even a commoner knew that such a timeless pastime as feeding one another was both a joy and responsibility.

This book brings you closer to a pure lifestyle and the practice of nonviolence, *ahimsa*, which is a prerequisite to yogic culture and vegetarianism even today. Just following any of the 108 recipes will naturally bring more physical and mental goodness, *sattva*, into your daily life. However, I also share stories about my pilgrimage around the table to feed the insightful, blissful part of you that is more hungry for enlightenment than for bread and sweets.

By taking you from the dining room of my childhood home to sitting cross-legged on the floor eating Indian *roti* (bread) with my hands today, I hope to share with you the morsels of mercy I have been blessed with in my culinary quest. If you find anything valuable on the way, I invite you to apply it to your life and pass it on to others.

My Kitchen Yoga

FROM MANNERS TO INTERACTION

The kitchen of the ashram was in the basement. Three-quarters of it was below ground level, and through a set of windows near the ceiling I could see shoes and trouser hems passing by on the sidewalk above. But my eyes fixed on what stood in front of me: a stove, sink, refrigerator, and countertops. The back wall held a mishmash of pots, pans, skillets, strainers, bowls, and trays. A row of hooks by the industrial oven had aprons, towels, and oven mitts hanging from them like ranks of uniforms. Although worn out, the terra-cotta tiles of the floor were immaculate. Steam danced from a stockpot of simmering milk, as if spinning a fable about the generosity of cows, grass, and earth. It wasn't the cheese making or the equipment or how expertly vegetables were chopped that changed how I perceived food; it was the character and wisdom of those who were cooking there. For the ashram cooks, every meal was a personal relationship and a gesture of love.

But the ashram appears much later in my story. I grew up in a family that ate dinner at the dining-room table every afternoon. And every Sunday until I went to college my mother made a special effort to prepare and serve a lunch on beautiful tableware. She knew how to cook and valued a nutritious

diet—we ate wholegrain bread in place of baguettes and fruit instead of candy.

Although my family's outlook on nutrition was pragmatic, the meal-time was dictatorial. I can't say for certain if we—my brother, parents, and I—ever chatted or laughed during the thousands of hours we faced one another at the table. We looked forward to filling our bellies and appreciated my mother's selfless contribution, but none of us explored the emotional—never mind the spiritual or devotional—potential of food. There was something awkward, even impaired, about sitting together.

For most of my childhood, I concentrated on becoming one with my chair and blending in with the table linens while properly holding my cutlery. Etiquette delineated the social boundaries and ambience—scooping the soup with a spoon in an outward movement and never slurping, poking, or shoveling food items or chewing with the mouth open, and certainly no talking while chewing or speaking unless spoken to. There was a lack of dynamic energy that would have enabled bonding and memorable exchanges within our tribe of four. Like so many people in modern society, we mistook the food items, silverware, good manners, and sheer coexistence for happiness, without understanding that these elements were there to create a framework for reciprocity and shared experiences. I learned to respect eating as much as I learned to respect people, but the mood was obedient or neutral at best.

At school it was different. In Finland formal education comes with a free daily buffet that you share with friends. The food wasn't nearly as tasty as my mom's (except for mashed potatoes with butter), but every time the bell rang at quarter to eleven, I was among the first children rushing to the cafeteria. Listening to and talking with my friends and, oh, constantly falling in love with boys supplied more nourishment than I could absorb.

As teenagers, my classmates and I skipped appetizers and went right to the main course, which was always a hearty and complex dish of dreams and worries. We never ruminated in silence if there was a confession or secret on the menu but gnawed on the subject to the last fiber, and afterward smacked our lips with delight. If for some reason we fell into mulling over a problem or utopian scheme, a side dish—usually a crunchy joke—snapped us out of it, as if to remind us there would always be a dessert to calm the palate and conclude the meal. Anything we ate was an excuse for juvenile drama! To drink, though, we always kept it simple and nourishing—milk, buttermilk, or water.

Gathering together to break bread at school with my friends, teachers, and the kitchen staff inspired me later to start a pop-up restaurant, called Stars and Atoms, in my living room when I was studying fine art at university. However, the ideal that my fellow students would bring raw ingredients that I would then transform into individualized meals perfectly suiting each student's constitution and humor proved to be over my head! I hardly could cook, and although eager, I was not good at reading people. The occasion quickly turned into a project that simply served food for thought—a salon, really.

We tackled philosophical dilemmas, argued about religion and politics, told true stories and tall tales alike, ridiculed everyone over thirty, solved world conflicts, and scrutinized historical figures from Napoleon to Gandhi, as if *monsieur* and *mahatma* themselves were munching beet casserole with us. Although many of the meals missed a culinary crescendo and the conversations caused heartburn, I felt connected to a community while dining. I got to know colorful people—some of whom I am still in touch with—and relished the companionship that comes with cooking for others.

As much as I wanted to align these two interests, food and people, I knew I would have to learn more about both, and about myself, to thrive. That desire eventually led me to the ashram kitchen and its terra-cotta tiles.

But before we return there, let me tell you about an incident that took place when I was nine years old. Although it is not directly related to food, it helps explain why I put away my paintbrushes for good, and why, two and half decades later, this book is called *Pure Vegetarian*.

THE ACCIDENT

I had just finished third grade. My plan to spend the summer holiday working at a stable, brushing and feeding horses, ended abruptly on the first morning there when the stud I was riding bolted on a quiet country road. Although my immediate reflex was to release the reins and slide off, for some reason I leaned forward and clenched the mane with both hands, until I blacked out and fell into a ditch.

Luckily the accident happened in front of the only house in the area. An elderly couple living there saw it through their kitchen window and called for an ambulance. My skull had fractured from ear to ear and forehead to neck like a coconut, and I was rushed to the emergency room.

I became aware of the situation at the hospital as I hovered above my bruised torso. My body lay like an empty shell on the bed. My mother stood next to it, hanging her head in shock, and when the doctor said, "The only thing we can do is to wait," she burst into tears.

From my perspective, I was dead and alive at the same time! Although I could see my body, I was unable to enter it. When a nurse pushed my hospital bed to a private room on the second afternoon, I followed while thinking, "This is *not* how I anticipated spending the school break!"

Trying to return to my body wore on me, and I was about to give up on the fifth or sixth day when, all of a sudden, the room filled with light. It felt like a blast had blown the windows open and the sun had erupted before my eyes. Blinded by the effulgence, I was sucked into a radiant tunnel. I wanted

to dive all the way through because it felt like the most soothing thing to do, but, to my disappointment, I then found myself back in my body.

I was able to move my fingers and toes again. I was sure someone had told me, "It is not your time to leave yet," but when I looked around, there was no one else in the room. I felt relaxed but had an overwhelming sense of duty, as if I had been granted a grave assignment. It only added to the burden I had carried since early childhood about who I really was and why I was born in a particular time, place, and circumstance. Three years prior— when I was only six years old—these kinds of questions had ushered me into a dialogue with what I envisioned and hoped to be God, although my parents had never exposed me to religion or prayer. However, now I felt daunted that my thirst for the holy might make me an advocate of sorts or, even worse, a priest in the future! I hesitated to speculate what my friends would say if they knew, and quickly pressed the call button next to the bed to alert the nurse's station, hoping to divert my unease with a glass of water.

As I recovered I never spoke about my out-of-body experience with the

doctors or my family, but it became a turning point that I returned to many times when I felt bewildered or lost throughout youth and adolescence. The accident changed the course of my identity, because from then on I knew I was neither a fragile anatomical structure nor just my thoughts and feelings. I had two bodies—physical and mental—that fit like a hand within a glove. The close-fitting outer layer, which most of us are so enamored of, seemed worthy only as long as it served functions like acquiring knowledge, touching objects, and achieving goals on command; whereas the ego, the mind, my sensitivities and longings seemed independent of the tissues, organs, and cells. This sense of myself felt linked to a greater energy source and could defy even death. Could that be true? None of these observations explained what the life force animating these bodies was and where my constant pursuit of happiness sprang from. I could only imagine what empowered the hand within the glove.

The search for the authentic self and the nature of being became my calling. Time and again I caught myself tracing patterns, relationships, and principles within forms, appearances, and situations in order to detect how details rely upon a greater context. It wasn't until I stumbled upon the seventeenth-century English poet and essayist John Donne's texts from the *Devotions* that I cast a glance at Eastern lore:

No man is an island
Entire of itself,
Every man is a piece of continent,
A part of the main.

When it was time to establish my life and career in mainstream society, I stretched beyond the Western mind-set and became, to the disapproval and resentment of my family, professors, and peers, a novice in an urban yoga hermitage (ashram), striving for simplicity and enlightenment. It was a decision that has shaped how I see everything in life today, and it diverted my food pilgrimage from an external to an internal path.

YOGA CUISINE

Ashram is a Sanskrit word for a place of self-realization. Sometimes it is used for a monastery or temple, but it also refers to any stage of life from student to household years and from retirement to renunciation when a person makes a deliberate effort to evolve as a spiritual being while performing his regular duties. This unique way of intertwining one's work and consciousness used to be the basis of Indian social structure, and is still an integral practice in the *bhakti* tradition from which the culinary inheritance of yoga cuisine originates and into which I was initiated in my early twenties. You could say that the ashram life is a culture of sacred living, because it transforms, among other things, a kitchen into a sanctum, cooking into meditation, and eating into a blessing.

Except for the fragrance of incense that became interlaced with the caramelized vapors of ghee, cumin, fennel, cinnamon, and chili in the kitchen, little changed in the environment and the basic routine of cooking. I still used a knife for chopping, a stove for boiling, and sugar for sweetening desserts. However, my state of mind sobered when I no longer viewed myself as a random cell, acting like a parasite that enjoys, controls, and exploits its host organism for selfish gain. Addressing the needs of the soul—not only mine but others', too—invoked a flavor I had never tasted before, and after discovering it, all other ways of eating, regardless of how attractive, aromatic, or refined they were, appeared flat and limited.

It gradually dawned on me that my interest in cooking had never really been about food—it had always been about fulfillment, which no amount of protein, fat, carbohydrates, vitamins, or minerals was able to bestow. Even the delight of sharing food with others, which I had held in higher esteem than gratifying the tongue, hadn't fully satiated my hunger until I linked food science, cooking techniques, and taste to transcendence. Perceiving and connecting all parts of reality—the soul, energies, and the energetic source—

made my manner and style of cooking a yoga practice. I started to observe food as energy that sustains both the temporary body (including the mind and intelligence) and the eternal soul, as if it were an electric current flowing from a power supply to simultaneously heat an oven and cool a refrigerator. That's when I found that food is a medium of affection and love, which you and I experience differently, according to our individual consciousness. Our capacity to taste is not constrained by the sophistication of the palate, social customs, or any other material condition, but it can reach beyond spiritual liberation into devotional bliss, which the soul is actually craving.

Some of the resident cooks in the temple I assisted for many years hadn't mastered recipe literacy, dexterity, or other mechanical skills, but they all displayed personal virtues like wisdom, kindness, truthfulness, self-control, humility, benevolence, and cleanliness to such a degree that it seemed like these attributes seasoned the food and touched everyone who took part. Their example showed that the attitude and characteristics affect the result as much as the physical facts and figures of gastronomy.

Many of the practices I adopted then I carry on still today, such as abstaining from onions, garlic, and mushrooms, which increase the tendencies for passionate and ignorant behavior; bathing before going to the kitchen; fasting from grains and pulses twice a month; and, foremost, offering everything we eat at home as a beautiful sacrament in our altar room by reciting Sanskrit hymns invoking auspiciousness. Food that is prepared and honored in such a way is called *prasadam,* or grace, and it not only frees us from the intricacies of *karma* (actions and reactions) and *samsara* (the repeated cycle of birth and death) but also facilitates interactions based on love.

PURE VEGETARIAN

Pure is an ambiguous term, but I have used it explicitly in the title of this book to draw your attention to the purity of consciousness, which *ahimsa,* or nonviolence—the cornerstone of vegetarianism—is built on. This is not my interpretation but a vision of Vedic seers, who believe that all living entities are essentially equal. Regardless of the varieties of embodiment, there is a godlike potency within every heart—human, animal, plant, and even a rudimentary insect, larva, fungus, germ, and microbe—that yearns to be acknowledged and illuminated.

To make educated choices is the higher license of humankind and comes with an obligation to ensure the well-being and advancement of those who depend on us. Unlike our four-legged friends, both you and I can question life's purpose, discriminate between spirit and matter, explore transcendental knowledge, and research the existence and relationships of the self and the Supreme before deciding what to have on a menu.

Purity is an active effort, and food presents unlimited opportunities to enforce it. I've noticed firsthand that sticking to fruits, vegetables, grains, nuts, sugar, water, and dairy products, which are fun to consume, easy to digest, and involve far less cruelty than a meat-based diet, harmonizes the lifestyle, attracts positive influences, and makes the mind receptive to a healthy sense of sacrifice, deep emotional presence, and philosophical thinking. Consuming only freshly prepared meals from the best-quality ingredients and keeping the surroundings uncluttered and peaceful encourage *sattva,* or balance, which is the natural disposition of the mind and a stepping-stone to the higher levels of consciousness.

I sincerely hope that my opening up about my food experience—which started as a fleeting sensation of joy that rushed through my mouth when a sweet union of flavors melted on my tongue, gradually melded into an expression of compassion and goodwill in the company of like-minded souls, and finally approached devotional contentment—will encourage you to discover new ways to understand yourself and your relationship with food.

part
One

RECIPES

ABOUT THE RECIPES

There are 108 beads in the rosary I meditate on every dawn. Because it is so close to my heart and symbolizes the most auspicious number of all Eastern faith traditions, I have selected 108 recipes and contemplated and cooked each one of them as gently and devotedly as I utter my morning prayers.

There are many directions I could have taken with the recipes because yoga cuisine is not limited to any particular ethnic kitchen. As I write this, my husband and I have just eaten cheese ravioli with butter and sage for lunch, and yesterday we wrapped chili in *masa harina* (corn flour) tortillas. But I would like to honor my spiritual roots that are deep in the Vedic tradition by sharing some of the preparations that have affected me in a special way over the years, knowing personally that Western vegetarianism has everything to gain from the versatility of Indian gastronomy. Also, in a cookbook I find it a good idea to focus on a single genre of cooking for the sake of literary harmony.

The recipes are not fully authentic because I am observing Indian food culture from the outside. While I am innovative with the ingredients, cooking techniques, and presentations, I lack access to the generations of gifted cooks, mothers, and aunts who would generously pass down the secrets of one of the strictest culinary traditions in the world. At the risk of seeming frivolous, I have plunged into South and North Indian, Maharashtrian, Gujarati, Bengali, and Oriya kitchens and absorbed their styles, knowing full well that each regional cuisine is distinct and usually portrayed separately. Regardless, I hope you will view each dish as if it were a tiny sprout growing from one person's research, enthusiasm, and bhakti-yoga lifestyle.

Like my meditation—like anyone's—these recipes are works in progress. Try to find the essence of each one; then imagine how some other vegetables, spices, or cooking methods would affect the color, taste, texture, scent, shape, and aroma. Whenever you find it suitable, play—feel free to roast the beetroots instead of boiling them, or use sweet potatoes in place of carrots or pumpkin, or vary the amounts of ghee, chili, spices, salt, and sugar. Take the list of ingredients and step-by-step instructions as guidelines and inspiration, but don't let them constrain your imagination. Once you understand the basic principle behind a recipe, you can personalize the details. When you optimize the recipes to suit your needs, you will find plenty of latitude to improvise, improve, and even perfect them!

Each recipe serves four people unless indicated otherwise. Take into consideration that every preparation is meant to be a part of a meal that would typically include at least rice and dal.

Food and Hospitality

Giving and receiving gifts, revealing the mind in confidence, and sharing a meal are some of the most powerful ways to show affection in everyday situations. Even if, for some reason, you are without friends and family, you can still make the best of the circumstance by accessing the universal network of love through meditation. Cooking is a great opportunity to learn about yourself and nature and to communicate with divinity. At best it is a reciprocal act in which you not only approach the divine but are also being seen. Whether you honor and serve food by yourself or with others, you always have a choice to make it a special event.

Although vastly underappreciated today, hospitality includes reception and entertainment of loved ones, guests, visitors, and even strangers. In European history showing respect and providing for the satisfaction of others determined a family's nobility and social standing. In India, however, the standards of being a host included treating guests as God, whether they were invited or arrived unannounced. This practice of *atithidevo bhava* is recorded in *Taittiriya Upanishad*, which dates back thousands of years and is still implemented to some extent in many communities regardless of economic means, local customs, and educational and professional background.

Said simply, selfless people derive pleasure from making others happy. Many times when I have been walking barefoot on a pilgrimage in the Indian countryside, villagers have opened their homes and hearts by offering clean water and piping-hot flatbread directly from the fire, along with sweets and fruits. According to the Vedic code of conduct, a householder should go outside and call very loudly to welcome anyone to eat before he and his family eat. Think about what a difference such a small gesture would make to everyone's life if more people practiced this! Whether you feed someone on a simple banana leaf or on an opulent silver platter is secondary to the gesture of service. The biological necessity of eating food will always be subordinate to its emotional, spiritual, and devotional impact.

Culture and Etiquette

Cleanliness is a luxury everyone can afford. In fact, everything that creates a pleasant atmosphere for a meal is free: appetite, fresh air, peaceful mind, light conversation, encouraging words, gratitude, and satisfaction. These qualities thrive on good habits: washing the hands, feet, and mouth before eating; wearing tidy clothes; sweeping the dining area before and after the meal; and reciting prayers. These are immediate ways to become purified inside and out, and when practiced, they gradually grow into values that change our lives for the better. We are all looking for life-altering results by

constantly acquiring knowledge but often forget that even the smallest gestures have the power to uplift and rejuvenate the body, mind, and soul.

The yogic etiquette differs from modern table manners in many ways. First of all, the floor is often used as a table! If you are healthy and flexible, and have a knack for *sukhasana* (easy pose) or *padmasana* (lotus posture), you will find it somewhat unnatural to sit on a chair again, because sitting cross-legged aligns the spine and musculoskeletal framework. You are in close contact with the earth's energy, which balances the nervous system. Bending forward to reach food and leaning back activates the abdominal muscles and increases the secretion of stomach acids. Also, when seated on the floor the blood flows more naturally through the heart to the digestive organs than when sitting in a chair, where the blood goes to the legs. And most significant, these seated postures calm the mind, which is the most important part of the body you want to keep jolly. If you don't appreciate what you eat, you won't be able to relish each mouthful or process the nutrients properly.

Sitting closely with others helps also to bond. If there are many people, line them up in rows or, if they are informal friends, in a circle so that everyone can have eye contact. By seating everyone comfortably on cushions you will be able to invite many more guests for a party even if you have a small apartment. You can always offer a chair and table for the elderly and those who have particular physical needs.

Instead of using different plates for an appetizer, entrée, and dessert, the types of meals I have presented in this book are usually served on large stainless-steel plates with a pinch of salt and pepper and a lemon wedge. You may also serve finely grated ginger on the side to increase the digestive fire. Of course, you can use ceramic tableware instead.

Set drinking glasses at the upper right side of the plate and place the spoons below them. There is no need for forks and knives; instead, I warmly encourage you to eat with the fingers of your right hand. Contrary to common belief, it is not unhygienic if you keep a normal standard of cleanliness. Touching food brings you in intimate contact with what you eat, and stimulates the digestive juices even before the food reaches the stomach. Using cutlery keeps the food at a distance, whereas using your fingers embraces it. This is a legacy from *mudra* tradition that utilizes hand gestures during worship and meditation, and in the culinary context emphasizes the sacred and mindful nature of eating. Each finger is a conduit of one of the five elements—space (*akash*), air, fire, water, and earth—and corresponds to a particular function of the micro- and macrocosmic body. The act of holding food between the thumb and fingers harmonizes these energies.

If you want to create a wonderful climate of gratitude and care around food, put others' well-being—including that of your house pets, if there are any—before your own. One way to do this is to remain standing and ready to grant anyone's wishes or needs by offering second and third helpings until their faces beam. You can eat and savor the meal after all your guests are sated.

Composing and Serving a Meal

If you are new to making Indian-style food, you may find it confusing to compose a meal. Use rice, dal, and some kind of bread—roti, puri, paratha, or a savory like singara—as the basis, and build a larger meal around these items by adding a vegetable dish, salad, chutney, and dessert. If you are hosting guests, you may want to serve two different kinds of rice and savory breads, multiple vegetable dishes, and two or three kinds of sweets.

It is better to eat a substantial breakfast and lunch and eat a lighter dinner. You may even skip dinner and eat just a snack in the afternoon. If you go to school or work outside of home, you may have to prepare the dinner later than ideal for the body.

I have written a few words about the recipes before the instructions, often indicating where the recipe comes from. When planning a menu, try to mix Bengali dishes with other Bengali dishes, and South Indian dishes with other South Indian dishes, and so on.

There are different customs for plating, but generally you serve hot rice with ghee and roti throughout the meal, whereas the rest of the items follow an order from lighter to richer. Consider that spicy foods activate the digestive juices and acids while sugar impedes them. If you cook Bengali or Oriya preparations, offer bitter tasting items (such as fried bitter melon) first; then spinach, dal, fritters, and vegetable dishes from dry to wet; and finally chutney before desserts.

At a meal drinking tends to distract the metabolism. According to

ayurveda it is best to drink water thirty minutes before or two hours after the meal. To maximize the health benefits, fill one-fourth of the belly with water and one-half of it with food, but leave one-quarter of the stomach empty.

Blessing

All these recipes offer you a chance to grow as a wholesome person, instead of just as a cook. It is up to you how far you want to reach and whether you want to address your attachment to cooking and eating as a union of taste buds and flavors, an opportunity for a loving interaction, or an alleviation of spiritual famine. In any case, I wish you a healthy appetite!

HOMEMADE DAIRY

Butter / 22

Ghee / 25

Sour Cream / 26

Sour Cream Dressing / 29

Cultured Buttermilk / 30

Crème Fraîche / 33

Homemade Yogurt / 34

Yogurt Cheese / 37

Takra (Churned Yogurt Drink) / 38

Savory Buttermilk Broth / 41

Chenna / Paneer (Fresh Pressed Cheese) / 42

Fried Cheese Balls / 45

Fried Cheese Cubes / 46

Butter

Homemade butter is quick and simple to make. The shelf life is shorter than that of a commercially produced butter, but freshly made, it has unparalleled flavor. Use it in cooking, baking, and candy making to add richness.

{MAKES ⅓ LB (160 G)}

2 cups cream (500 ml),
   35–40% fat
2 cups (500 ml) ice-cold
   water, or as needed

Place the cream in a food processor and process it until it gradually transforms from a thick, whipped cream into granular butter and buttermilk. Transfer the mixture to a clean, large bowl and add a half of the ice-cold water. Press it with a spatula to extract as much buttermilk as possible. When the butter becomes a solid mass, pour the excess liquid (buttermilk) into another container and save it for drinking, cooking, or baking. Add the rest of the water and press the butter again with a spatula to extract more liquid. Finally, place the butter on a sieve and strain out any excess buttermilk.

Wrap the butter in parchment paper or place it in a lidded container. Butter can be stored in the refrigerator for 1 to 3 weeks, depending on how thoroughly the buttermilk has been removed. Any residual buttermilk will sour the butter in time.

Ghee

*Smaller amounts of ghee are conveniently made on the stovetop, whereas larger amounts
are made effortlessly in the oven. I usually make ghee once a month from 2 kilograms of butter.
Golden and sattvic, in the mode of goodness, it imparts unparalleled aroma to both the food
and the kitchen. The finest quality ghee comes from homemade butter. You can make seasoned ghee easily
by simmering spices, such as black pepper or ginger, along with the butter.*

{MAKES ABOUT 3 CUPS (800 G)}

2¼ lbs (1 kg) butter

Slice 1 kilogram butter thinly and place it in a wide, heavy-bottomed pan or casserole over a moderately low temperature. Always leave two-thirds of the pan empty for the butter to splatter.

When the butter has melted, increase the heat to moderate and bring it to a boil. Immediately reduce the heat to minimum and simmer, uncovered and undisturbed, until the milk solids separate. Use a slotted spoon to skim the whitish foam or thin crust from the top of the ghee. Set it aside in a small bowl or jar for later use in a batter or dough when baking.

From time to time, gently shake the pan to prevent the solids on the bottom from burning. At no point should they be darker than light golden.

The ghee is ready when there is a thin, transparent crust on the top, a clear golden layer of butterfat in the middle, and a golden crust on the bottom. The fragrance should be mild and pleasant. It will take about 2 hours to simmer 1 kilogram of butter.

Turn off the heat. Let the ghee stand for a while and then remove any crust from the surface with a spoon. Ladle off as much ghee as you can without disturbing the solids on the bottom and pour the ghee into a clean, dry jar through a fine sieve, filter, or muslin cloth.

Let the ghee cool completely before closing the lid of the jar. Store the ghee at room temperature; it will remain unspoiled for months and will have a fudgelike consistency. Refrigerated, it becomes a solid block. Always scoop the ghee with a dry, clean spoon.

Pour the remaining butterfat into another jar. It can be used in cooking and baking. Stored in a refrigerator, it should be used within a couple of days.

Sour Cream

Sour cream is primarily used in European and North American cuisine as a condiment, dressing, or cooking and baking ingredient. I often substitute it for cream to add a lighter and pleasantly sour taste. In addition, it makes yogurt-based dishes richer. Add sour cream at the end of cooking; otherwise, it will curdle if it's brought to a boil.

{MAKES 2 CUPS (500 ML)}

2 cups (500 ml) light cream, 10–20% fat

1–2 Tbsp natural yogurt (with live culture), preferably organic

Heat the cream in a pot to just before the boiling point (176°F [80°C]). Remove the pot from the heat and let the cream cool, mixing it occasionally, until it reaches around 100°F (38°C), or just about body temperature. When making larger amounts of sour cream, you can speed up the process by placing the pot in a bowl of cold water.

When the temperature is ideal, transfer the cream to a ceramic or glass jar. Add the yogurt. Mix the cream gently and cover the jar loosely with a lid or plastic film. Place it in a warm, draft-free location for 6 to 12 hours. The fermenting success and time depend on the strength of the culture and the cleanliness, temperature, and humidity of your home.

When the sour cream settles, cover and store it in the refrigerator. Use it within 3 to 4 days.

Sour Cream Dressing

This quick, simple dressing makes an ideal complement for steamed vegetables,
salads, savory snacks, and breads. Garnish it with fresh herbs, like cilantro,
dill, or parsley.

{MAKES 2 CUPS (500 ML)}

Whisk all ingredients except the herbs by hand until smooth. Just before serving, fold in the herbs.

Store the dressing covered in the refrigerator for 2 to 3 days.

2 cups (500 ml) homemade sour cream (page 26)
3 Tbsp extra virgin olive oil
1 tsp freshly ground black pepper
1 tsp mustard seeds, powdered
1 tsp curry powder
½ tsp hing powder
½ tsp turmeric powder
1 tsp black salt
1 tsp sea salt, or to taste
1 tsp organic whole cane sugar
6 Tbsp lemon juice
Handful of fresh herbs, chopped (optional)

Cultured Buttermilk

Rich and creamy cultured buttermilk is a pleasantly sour base for soups, gravies, and drinks.
For baking, whether breads or cakes, it acts as a mediator and binds the ingredients together.
It reacts well with a rising agent, such as baking soda, and produces light and airy pastries.

{MAKES 4 CUPS (1 LITER)}

4 cups (1 liter) organic milk,
  4% fat
2 Tbsp cultured buttermilk

Combine the milk and cultured buttermilk in a glass or ceramic jar. Mix the ingredients well, cover the jar loosely with a lid or plastic film, and set it to rest in a warm, draft-free place for 8 to 12 hours. The fermenting success and time depend on the strength of the culture and the cleanliness, temperature, and humidity in your home.

When the buttermilk is settled, keep it covered and store it in the refrigerator.

There is a thin layer of cream on the top of the buttermilk when you make it from organic milk that is pasteurized but not homogenized. You may spoon it out and use it in cooking and baking, or you can whisk and mix it with the rest of the buttermilk. You can make buttermilk from milk with a lower fat content, too.

Crème Fraîche

As a thicker fermented product with a higher fat content than sour cream, crème fraîche tolerates boiling without curdling. It has a tangy, almost nutty flavor. You can also whip it to top cakes and desserts. Crème fraîche accompanies any soups and steamed vegetables.

{MAKES 1 CUP (250 ML)}

Bring the cream and the buttermilk to room temperature. Combine the ingredients well in a ceramic or glass container. Cover the container loosely with a lid or plastic film, and set the mixture to rest in a warm, draft-free place for 24 to 36 hours. The fermenting success and duration depend on the strength of the culture and the cleanliness, temperature, and humidity in your home.

When the crème fraîche is thickened and set, store it in a lidded jar in the refrigerator, where it will continue to thicken and mature. It will keep for a week.

1 cup (250 ml) cream, 35–40% fat
1–2 Tbsp cultured buttermilk (page 30)

Homemade Yogurt

*Yogurt culture, a living bacteria, is used to ferment the lactose of milk
in order to produce lactic acid, which in turn acts on milk protein
and gives yogurt its characteristic texture and tang.*

{MAKES 4 CUPS (1 LITER)}

4 cups (1 liter) organic milk,
4% fat
1 Tbsp natural yogurt
(with live culture)

Bring the milk to a boil in a pot over moderate heat. As soon as it boils, remove it from the heat and let it cool until it's cool enough to touch for 5 to 6 seconds without burning. An ideal temperature is around 113°F (45°C). Pour the milk into a ceramic or glass container, add the yogurt, cover the mixture loosely, and let it rest for 6 to 8 hours or overnight in a warm, draft-free place. The fermenting success and time depend on the strength of the culture and the cleanliness, temperature, and humidity of your home.

As soon as the yogurt settles, place it in a clean container and store it in the refrigerator. Keeping it at room temperature longer than necessary will sour it.

There is a thin layer of cream on the top of the yogurt when you make it from organic milk that is pasteurized but not homogenized. You may spoon it out to use in cooking and baking, or you may whisk and mix it with the rest of the yogurt. You can make yogurt from milk with a lower fat content, too.

Yogurt Cheese

*This recipe yields creamy, soft cheese that is made by straining yogurt through a cloth
to remove whey. It is a traditional cheese in the Levant and the Arabian Peninsula
but is also found in Central Asia and the Indian Subcontinent.*

*Smear it as a dip or spread on a flatbread, or use it in cooking to add flavor and texture. Add salt,
spices, and herbs and roll it into a log or sprinkle it with finely chopped nuts and olive oil. See the recipes
for batter-fried yogurt cheese balls, pakora, and a saffron-infused dessert, shrikhand, which follow.*

{MAKES ABOUT 1 ½ CUPS (375 ML)}

Transfer the yogurt to a sieve or colander lined with a large, thin cotton cloth. If the cloth is too thin, you may want to double the thickness. Otherwise, the cloth will pass through the curd along with the whey without separating them.

Wrap the cloth around the yogurt and suspend it with string or twine in the refrigerator for 12 to 18 hours. Remember to place a bowl underneath it to collect the whey.

After 12 to 18 hours, remove the cloth bag from the refrigerator and peek in to see how dry it is. Mix the yogurt with a spoon or spatula, suspend the cloth again with a string or twine, and let it strain in the refrigerator until the yogurt reaches a desired consistency. It may take up to 36 hours for the yogurt to firm up completely.

Use the whey instead of water in baking and cooking. It's nutritious and tasty.

Keep the yogurt in the refrigerator while and after fermentation; otherwise, it will sour. Stored in the refrigerator, yogurt cheese keeps for about one week.

8 cups (2 liters) yogurt
(page 34)

Takra

(Churned Yogurt Drink)

A Sanskrit word, takra refers to gently sour and astringent fermented milk from which butter has been removed. According to ayurveda, takra has healing properties. It kindles the digestive fire without creating acid, which makes it particularly beneficial for those with intestinal irregularities, such as bloating, hemorrhoids, colitis, irritable bowel syndrome, or diarrhea. Takra increases the appetite, so drink 1 cup of it on an empty stomach 1 hour before a meal.

{MAKES 5–6 CUPS (1.25–1.5 LITERS)}

4 cups (1 liter) organic milk, 4% fat

1 Tbsp natural yogurt (with live culture)

1–2 cups (250–500 ml) ice-cold water

Bring the milk to a boil in a pot over moderate heat. As soon as it boils, remove it from the heat and let it cool until it's cool enough to touch for 5 to 6 seconds without burning your finger. An ideal temperature is around 113°F (45°C). Pour the milk into a ceramic or glass container, add the yogurt, cover it loosely, and let it rest for 6 to 8 hours or overnight in a warm, draft-free place. The fermenting success and time depend on the strength of the culture and the cleanliness, temperature, and humidity of your home.

As soon as the yogurt settles, place it in a food processor along with 1 cup (250 ml) ice-cold water.

Because the yogurt is made from organic milk, which is not homogenized, there is a layer of cream on top. When you process the yogurt with ice-cold water, the cream will turn into granulates of butter that cling to the top of the yogurt. If the cream doesn't turn into butter within 5 minutes of processing, add more ice water through the feed tube. Turn off the food processor when you clearly see yellow granulates of butter on the surface of the diluted yogurt.

You can also churn the butter manually by vigorously swiveling the handle of a whisk between your palms while simultaneously lifting it in an up and down motion. It takes about 10 minutes to separate the butter by hand.

Skim the butter from the top of the *takra*. There won't be more than a good tablespoon of butter. Once you have removed it, pour the takra through a fine sieve to separate all the remaining particles of butter. Now the takra is ready for drinking or to be used in cooking. Store it in a covered container in a refrigerator and use it within 3 to 4 days.

Savory Buttermilk Broth

Homemade cultured buttermilk is the key ingredient of this broth. It has a round, soft
flavor much like yogurt (which can be used as a substitute, too). If you are unaccustomed
to eating with your fingers, this recipe offers a good start. I love to dunk urad-dal doughnuts,
boiled potatoes, or roasted okra in it or ladle it over plain rice. You become
more conscious of what you eat when you touch and feel each handful.

{MAKES 4 CUPS (1 LITER)}

Beat the buttermilk, turmeric, cayenne, sugar, and salt in a bowl until the mixture is light and smooth. Set it aside.

Dry roast the coriander and fenugreek seeds in a skillet or pan over a moderately low temperature until they turn a few shades darker and aromatic, about 5 to 6 minutes. Remove the pan from the heat and combine the dry roasted ingredients with the coconut, cashew nuts, chilies, and water in an electric spice mill or mortar. Grind the ingredients to a paste and add it to the buttermilk.

Bring the whipped buttermilk to a boil in a heavy-bottomed pot over moderate heat, constantly stirring it with a wooden spatula. Then, reduce the heat to low. Keep stirring for 5 minutes, then turn off the heat.

Heat the ghee or oil in a small sauté pan over moderate heat until it's hot but not smoking. Add the mustard and jeera seeds. As soon as the mustard seeds turn gray and pop, add the crushed curry leaves and hing. Then, pour the spices into the buttermilk. Mix, cover, and let the flavors steep for at least 5 minutes before serving.

FOR THE BUTTERMILK
4 cups (1 liter) cultured
  buttermilk, at room
  temperature (page 30)
½ tsp turmeric powder
½ tsp cayenne powder
1 tsp sugar
1 tsp sea salt, or to taste

FOR THE SPICE-NUT PASTE
1½ tsp coriander seeds
¼ tsp fenugreek seeds
6 Tbsp fresh, finely grated
  coconut
20 cashew nuts
2–3 green chilies, seeded
½ cup (125 ml) hot water, or
  as needed

FOR THE TEMPERING
1–2 Tbsp ghee or oil
½ tsp black mustard seeds
½ tsp jeera seeds
8–10 small fresh curry leaves,
  crushed
¼ tsp hing powder

Chenna / Paneer
(Fresh Pressed Cheese)

*This recipe makes cloud-white cottage cheese, which is then pressed under a
weight to make paneer. Perhaps the simplest type of unripened cheese,
paneer is used abundantly throughout South Asia—and abundantly in my kitchen, too.*

*My tips for pressing perfect paneer are these: choose full-fat, organic milk;
use clean utensils and pans; boil the milk over moderate heat; use as little curdling agent
(such as lemon juice) as possible; stir the milk gently; remove the pan from the heat
immediately after the milk has curdled; and press the cheese shortly thereafter.*

{MAKES 16 OZ (450 G) CHENNA AND 12 OZ (335 G) PANEER}

¼ cup (63 ml) water
12 cups (3 liters) organic milk,
  4% fat
3–4 Tbsp lemon juice,
  or as needed

Bring the water to a boil in a medium-size, heavy-bottomed pan
over high heat. As soon as it boils, reduce the heat to moderate and
add the milk. Cook the liquid for 15 to 20 minutes, stirring often to
prevent scorching, until it reaches the boiling point. Add the lemon
juice, 1 tablespoon at a time, gently stirring between additions.
After 3 tablespoons, if the milk has not curdled, add the juice drop
by drop. The exact amount of lemon juice you will need to curdle
the milk depends on the fat content of milk and how sour the
lemons are. Use as little juice as it takes to separate the cheese. The
whey should have a light greenish color.

Remove the pan from the heat and transfer the cheese with a
slotted spoon to a sieve or colander lined with a large, thin cotton
cloth. Place a bowl underneath to collect the whey.

This cheese mass is called *chenna,* or soft cottage cheese. You can
spread it on a sandwich with spices and herbs, or knead it into a silky
smooth paste that looks like cream cheese. Chenna is used especially
for making sweets, like chhena-poda, kalakand, and sandesh. It is
also the main ingredient of fried cheese balls, on page 45.

Keep chenna in a sealed box in the refrigerator and use it within
2 to 3 days.

How to Make Paneer

If you want to cut the cheese into cubes to be used in cooking, it must first be pressed under a weight. As such, it's called *paneer*.

When it is still warm and soft, turn the cheese out onto a cheesecloth. Wrap and fold the edges of the cloth tightly around the cheese. Transfer the bundle to a clean platter or tray and place a weight, such as a pot filled with water, on top of it for no longer than 5 to 7 minutes. This will force out any excess whey and leave the paneer firm yet succulent.

Paneer can be stored in a sealed box in the refrigerator for 3 to 4 days.

Fried Cheese Balls

Messy to fry, cheese balls are nevertheless the center of attention whenever they are served.
I've yet to meet someone who doesn't like them! Cheese made from organic milk yields the softest,
most indulgent result. Add cheese balls to any vegetable preparation, salad, or rice dish
to create contrast and interest. In a sauce made of tomato or sour cream, they soak up the juices,
expand, and explode in the mouth! For a snack, try them with tomato chutney.

{MAKES 18–20 CHEESE BALLS}

Make the cheese from 12 cups (3 liters) of milk according to the instructions on page 42. Strain the cheese in a sieve, for 20 minutes to 1 hour. Place the strained cheese in the food processor and process until it forms a solid mass that is smooth and without graininess. Transfer it to a kitchen counter.

Roll the cheese into a log and divide it into 18 to 20 portions. Roll each one into a smooth ball between your palms or against the kitchen counter. Then, dip the balls in the flour and coat them evenly.

Add enough ghee or oil to a pan or wok to fully cover the balls during frying. Heat the ghee or oil over moderate heat. Remember to leave at least one-third of the wok empty. Deep frying makes the surface bubble and sputter.

When the ghee or oil is hot but not smoking, slide the cheese balls, one by one, down the sides of the pan. Fry them in batches without overcrowding the pan. Move them in the ghee or oil with a slotted spoon. When they turn golden brown, remove them and drain them in a colander or on paper towels.

Fried cheese balls are delicate, so add them to wet dishes, such as the beans and cheese balls in tomato sauce on page 111 toward the end of cooking. Otherwise, they may disintegrate.

16 oz (450 g) chenna or
fresh cheese (page 42)
All-purpose flour, for dusting
Ghee (page 25) or oil,
for frying

Fried Cheese Cubes

Fried paneer cubes hide a soft, moist heart under a crunchy exterior.
You can add them to vegetable dishes, soups, and curries.
They substantiate salads too and provide a good source of protein in a meal.

{MAKES 2 CUPS (500 ML)}

12 oz (335 g) paneer
  (page 42)
1–2 Tbsp ghee
  (page 25) or oil,
  plus more for frying
½ tsp jeera seeds
2" (5 cm) piece of cinnamon
  stick
4 cardamom pods
4 cloves
1 dry red chili, crushed
1 tsp coriander powder
½ tsp freshly ground black
  pepper
¼ tsp turmeric
¼ tsp hing powder
3 cups (750 ml) whey
½ tsp kala namak powder
1–2 tsp sea salt, or to taste

Make and press paneer from 12 cups (3 liters) of milk according to the instructions on page 42. When it has been under a weight for 5 to 7 minutes, unwrap the cheese and cut it into 1-inch (2.5 cm) cubes. Collect the whey in a bowl and set it aside.

While the cheese is under the weight, heat the ghee or oil in a wok or pot over moderate heat. When it's hot but not smoking, add the jeera seeds, cinnamon stick, cardamom pods, cloves, and crushed chili. Fry them for 30 seconds, tossing and turning the spices with a spatula, then add the coriander, black pepper, turmeric, and hing powder, immediately followed by the whey. Sprinkle the mixture with kala namak powder and salt. Bring the liquid to a boil over moderately low heat.

Now, heat at least 1 inch (2.5 cm) ghee or oil in another pan or wok over high heat. When it's hot but not smoking, reduce the heat to moderate and slip the cheese cubes in, carefully, with the help of a slotted spoon. Fry them—constantly turning them gently so they don't break—until they are reddish golden on all sides. Transfer them to the pot with the boiling whey. Reduce the heat to the lowest possible setting and simmer them for 5 to 10 minutes.

Serve the cheese cubes with any steamed vegetables, salads, or tomato chutney, or add them to, for example, the Brussels sprouts in cream on page 96 or pumpkin and spinach on page 123. You can use the spiced whey in place of water for cooking plain rice.

SPICES

Ground Sweet Neem (Curry Leaf Powder) / 50

Curry Powder / 53

Sambar Powder / 54

Panch Phoron / 57

Garam Masala / 58

Chaat Masala / 61

Ground Sweet Neem

(Curry Leaf Powder)

*Sweet neem leaves are better known as curry leaves or kadi patta. They are highly valued in
South Indian cuisine for their aromatic and medicinal properties. The taste is earthy and mildly bitter.
Fresh leaves have a short shelf life and lose their delicate fragrance quickly.
Always fry them briefly in hot ghee, butter, or oil to enhance the taste and bring out their crispy texture.*

*If you don't have access to fresh curry leaves year-round, buy a large bunch from an
Asian grocery in high season, and dry roast and coarsely powder them for later use.
I always have a jar of sweet neem powder in the pantry and sprinkle a teaspoon of it whenever
a recipe asks to temper 8 to 10 fresh leaves in ghee or oil.*

{MAKES 7 OZ (200 G)}

7 oz (200 g) fresh curry leaves
Pinch of salt (optional)

Wash and drain the leaves. Spread them on a kitchen towel to air dry overnight.

The next day, roast them lightly in a skillet or pan over low heat, tossing and turning the spices with a spatula for 3 to 4 minutes until the leaves become slightly brown. Take care not to burn the leaves!

Remove the leaves from the skillet to let them cool. Then, grind them into powder. You may add salt, but it's optional. Store the leaves in an airtight container and use them within a month or two in the recipes that call for fresh curry leaves when none is available.

Curry Powder

Curry powder is perhaps the most common masala, or spice mix, associated with Indian cooking in the West. However, it's a remnant of the British Raj, or domination, and most Indian cooks don't even know about it! Curry powder was designed to create an "Indian flavor" with minimal effort. Some varieties of South Indian sambar and rasam masala could be interpreted as the closest it gets to curry powder. Because it's so widely used in the West, I'm offering two homemade versions. The first one is simple, and the latter provides more complex flavors. They are interchangeable in recipes.

Variation 1

{MAKES ABOUT ¾ CUP (188 ML)}

Dry roast the coriander, jeera, fennel, and chilies in a skillet or pan over moderately low heat, tossing and turning the spices with a spatula, until the spices become a few shades darker and aromatic, for 5 to 6 minutes. Be careful not to burn them!

Remove the skillet from the heat and transfer the spices to a platter or plate. If you leave the spices on the hot pan, they will continue roasting.

When the spices are at room temperature, grind them in a spice mill or mortar and add the turmeric powder.

4 Tbsp coriander seeds
2 Tbsp jeera seeds
2 Tbsp fennel seeds
3–4 dried red chilies
2 Tbsp turmeric powder

Variation 2

{MAKES 1 CUP (250 ML)}

Dry roast the jeera, mustard, fenugreek, urad dal, black peppercorns, red chilies, and curry leaves as instructed in Variation 1. When they are a few shades darker and aromatic, remove the pan from the heat, let the spices cool, and grind them into a powder along with the (unroasted) coriander seeds. Finally, add the turmeric powder.

Store the curry powder in an airtight container away from heat and light. All powdered spices lose their potency if they are stocked for long periods of time. Therefore, it's recommended to make small portions at a time.

1½ Tbsp jeera seeds
1½ Tbsp mustard seeds
1 tsp fenugreek seeds
1 tsp urad dal
2 tsp black peppercorns
3–4 dried red chilies
Handful of fresh curry leaves
4 Tbsp coriander seeds
2 Tbsp turmeric powder

Sambar Powder

Sambar is a vegetable stew based on a broth made typically of toor dal, tamarind, and a particular spice mix or masala. Cinnamon isn't traditionally a part of sambar powder, although it's often found in commercial products. I've included cinnamon here because it works well with the eggplant sambar recipe in this book. You can also toss in sambar masala as a general spice mix whenever you want to season plain rice, dal, or a vegetable dish.

{MAKES ABOUT 1 CUP (250 ML)}

1 tsp oil
4 Tbsp coriander seeds
1 Tbsp jeera seeds
½ tsp black peppercorns
1 Tbsp channa dal
2–4 dried red chilies
1" (2.5 cm) stick of cinnamon, crushed
½ tsp fenugreek
½ cup (125 ml) desiccated coconut

Combine all the ingredients except for the coconut in a skillet or pan over moderately low heat tossing and turning the spices with a spatula for 5 or 6 minutes until the spices turn slightly darker and release a pleasant aroma. Be careful not to burn them!

Toward the end of cooking, add the coconut. Remove the skillet from the heat and transfer the spices to a platter or plate as soon as the coconut turns light golden. If you leave the spices on the hot pan, they will continue roasting.

When the spices are at room temperature, grind them in a spice mill or mortar. Store the sambar powder in an airtight container away from heat and light. All powdered spices lose their potency if they are stocked for a long period of time. Therefore, it's recommended to make small portions at a time.

Panch Phoron

Panch phoron is a classic Bengali spice mix and one of my favorite choices to season almost any vegetable dish or chutney. It offers contrasting flavors: the mustards seeds are smoky, fenugreek is pleasantly bitter, jeera is earthy, fennel is sweet, and kalonji is fresh. You can briefly fry the spices in hot ghee or oil, or if you want to hide the texture, dry roast and then grind the seeds into powder.

Bengali and Odisha cooks use radhuni in place of mustard seeds, but being a rare spice, radhuni is hardly available outside of India. It is a relative of another seed, ajwain, whose sharp scent resembles a mixture of anise, thyme, and oregano. In my opinion, mustard seeds are easier on the Western palate.

{MAKES 5 TBSP (175 G)}

Combine the seeds and store them in an airtight container away from heat and light. You can use this base recipe and ratio for mixing a larger amount of panch phoron for later use. When you want to season a dish with it, take the amount the recipe calls for, and temper it in hot ghee or oil until the mustard seeds pop and turn gray.

Alternatively, dry roast the spices in a skillet or pan over moderately low heat, tossing and turning the spices with a spatula for 5 to 6 minutes until the spices turn a few shades darker and aromatic. Be careful not to burn the seeds!

Remove the pan from the heat and let the seeds cool. Grind them into powder.

Store the panch phoron in an airtight container away from heat and light.

1 Tbsp fennel seeds
1 Tbsp fenugreek seeds
1 Tbsp jeera seeds
1 Tbsp kalonji seeds
1 Tbsp black mustard seeds

Garam Masala

The composition of garam masala differs regionally, which means the variety is as wide as there are cooks in India. Although typical to North Indian cuisine, garam masala has become popular across the continent as well as internationally. Add it to a dish at the end of cooking to preserve its aroma. You can lightly dust almost any savory dish with garam masala when you want to introduce warmth and sweetness to contrast pungency and saltiness.

{MAKES 4–5 TBSP}

1 Tbsp jeera seeds
1 Tbsp coriander seeds
10 cloves
10 green cardamom pods,
 lightly crushed
2" (5 cm) piece cinnamon
1 tsp sesame seeds (optional)
Tiny piece of nutmeg

Dry roast the ingredients in a skillet or pan over moderately low heat, tossing and turning the spices with a spatula, for 5 to 6 minutes until they turn a few shades darker and aromatic. Be careful not to burn them!

Remove the skillet from the heat and transfer the spices to a platter or plate. If you leave the spices on the hot pan, they will continue roasting.

When the spices are at room temperature, grind them in a spice mill or mortar.

Store garam masala in an airtight container away from heat and light. For a more refined taste, you may remove the green cardamom husks after frying the spices and grind only the tiny black seeds.

Chaat Masala

I always have chaat masala ready to be sprinkled over hot rice, fresh cheese, salads, chutneys, or fried food. This spice mix pairs well with roti, paratha, and poori alike and gives the little bit of extra flavor to elevate any dish.

{MAKES ABOUT 7 TBSP}

Dry roast the jeera seeds in a skillet or pan over moderate to moderately low heat, tossing and turning the spices with a spatula, until they become a few shades darker and aromatic, for 5 to 6 minutes. Remove the pan from the heat and let the seeds cool. Grind them into powder.

Combine the jeera powder, black pepper, amchoor, kala namak, and hing. Store the mixture in an airtight container at room temperature.

1 Tbsp jeera seeds
2 tsp freshly ground black pepper
2½ Tbsp amchoor powder
2 Tbsp kala namak powder
¼ tsp hing powder

RICE, GRAINS & DAL

Basic Dal / 64

Basmati Rice / 67

Coconut Rice with Saffron / 68

Lemon Rice with Cashews / 71

Green Mung Dal with Fennel / 72

Jagannath Dal / 75

Green Mango Dal / 76

Kitchari (Rice and Dal Porridge) / 79

Quinoa Kitchari / 80

Eggplant Lentil Sambar with Curry Leaves / 83

Upma / 84

Basic Dal

For me, dal is part of a balanced diet with rice and vegetables. It's hard to imagine life without it.
I modify this base recipe daily to accommodate the rest of the menu, season, company, or occasion. You can
add unlimited combinations of spices and vegetables to it. In this way, dal always appears new and exciting.

Although yellow split mung dal cooks in 15 to 20 minutes on a stove, and even more quickly in a pressure
cooker, it is better to reserve 30 to 40 minutes for boiling it to make the dal more digestible.

By increasing or decreasing the amount of water, you can adjust how thick you want the dal to be.

{SERVES 4}

FOR THE DAL
8 cups (2 liters) water
1 cup (250 ml) yellow split
  mung dal
Dab of ghee (page 25),
  butter, or oil
½ tsp turmeric powder
2–3 tomatoes

FOR THE TEMPERING
1–2 Tbsp ghee or oil
1 Tbsp grated ginger
  (juice removed)
1 tej patta
½ tsp jeera seeds
1 fresh green chili, split
¼ tsp freshly ground black
  pepper
⅓ tsp hing powder
2½ tsp sea salt, or to taste

TO SERVE
1–2 Tbsp lemon juice
Handful (20 g) of fresh
  cilantro, chopped

Sort, wash, and drain the dal. Set it aside.

Bring the water to a boil in a medium to large pot over high heat. When it is boiling, reduce the heat to moderate and add the dal. As soon as a layer of foam appears on the top, remove the foam (froth) with a spoon and add a dab of ghee, butter, or oil, and turmeric. Cover the pot and cook the mixture for 20 minutes, occasionally stirring. You may want to keep the lid ajar at first because the dal tends to boil over.

In the meantime, wash, peel, and remove the stems from the tomatoes. Quarter them and set them aside.

When the dal has cooked for 20 minutes, add the tomatoes. Cook the mixture for another 15 to 20 minutes until the dal has dissolved and the tomatoes are very soft. Mix the dal every 4 or 5 minutes during cooking. Then, turn off the heat. Whisk the dal to make it smooth.

Make the tempering by heating up the ghee or oil in a small pan or pot over moderate heat. When it's hot but not smoking, add the grated ginger (juice removed) and tej patta. Fry the ginger until it is light golden. Add the jeera seeds and sauté the ingredients for 20 seconds, tossing and turning the spices with a spatula. Then add the chili, black pepper, and hing powder. Pour the tempering into the dal.

Add the salt. Let the flavors steep for at least 5 minutes before serving. Garnish with lemon juice and fresh cilantro.

Basmati Rice

Basmati rice can be prepared several ways. After making basmati rice the same way for twenty years, I recently discovered that washing, soaking, and boiling rice in plenty of water for only 7 minutes then draining and letting it stand, covered, for 10 to 15 minutes, yields a better result. When properly cooked, it's light and fluffy, providing a neutral canvas with a firm texture for the rest of the meal. For the best digestive and culinary experience, basmati rice should be served with a spoonful of ghee or butter. Measure a handful (¼ cup [63 ml]) of uncooked rice per person as a side dish.

{SERVES 4}

Sort the rice and remove any small stones or impurities. Wash and drain it at least three times with plenty of water until the water is clear. Soak it in clean water for 20 to 30 minutes. Soaking makes a difference in the final texture; therefore, don't skip this step.

Bring the water to a boil in a pan or pot over high heat.

Drain the rice and add it to the boiling water. Mix it with a spoon, reduce the heat to moderate, and boil the rice for 7 minutes. Then turn off the heat, drain the rice, and return it to the pot. Pour in the lemon juice now, if you want to use it. Place the pot on a warm electric stove, or if you have a gas burner, a minimum flame. Alternatively, you can place the pot in a warm oven. Cover the pot and let the rice rest for 10 to 15 minutes.

Uncover the rice, add the salt and ghee, butter, or oil, and mix the rice gently with a fork or spoon before serving.

1 cup (250 ml) basmati rice
About 8 cups (2 liters) water
1 Tbsp lemon juice (optional)
½ tsp sea salt, or to taste
1–2 Tbsp ghee (page 25), butter, or oil

Coconut Rice with Saffron

Coconut rice can be made as elaborate or simple as desired, yet it is always soothing.
It is goodness personified. With a soft saffron hue, it looks stunning.

{SERVES 4}

1 cup (250 ml) basmati rice
Half of 1 fresh coconut,
　divided
1½ cup (375 ml) hot water
Pinch of saffron threads
1 Tbsp hot water
Pinch of sugar
1 tsp sea salt, or to taste

FOR THE TEMPERING
1–2 Tbsp ghee (page 25) or oil
2" (5 cm) piece of cinnamon
4 whole green cardamom
　pods, lightly crushed
½ tsp coarsely ground black
　pepper
Pinch of hing
1 Tbsp lemon juice

TO SERVE
½ cup (125 ml) small currants

Sort, wash, and drain the rice. Set aside.

Remove the outer shell and the thin, brown skin of the coconut. Split the half coconut in two equal pieces; process one piece of the coconut and hot water in a blender until it becomes a white paste. Strain the milk and set it aside. Save the pulp for a later use in cooking or baking.

Toast the saffron in a dry pan or skillet over moderate heat for about 30 seconds until it crumbles when you crush it with your fingers. Remove it from the heat and dissolve it in a spoonful of hot water. Pour the saffron water into the coconut milk and add the sugar and salt, too.

Heat the ghee or oil in a pot over moderate heat. When it's hot but not smoking, add the cinnamon and cardamom. Fry the spices for 30 seconds then add the black pepper and hing powder immediately followed by the rice. Sauté the ingredients for a couple minutes until some of the grains become transparent and some of them turn white. Add the coconut milk. As soon as it comes to a boil, reduce the heat to minimum, cover the pot, and simmer the rice for 15 minutes without stirring.

Turn off the heat and pour the lemon juice over the rice. Cover it again and let it sit for 10 to 15 minutes before stirring it. To tell if the rice is cooked, remove a grain and squeeze it with your fingers. It should mash easily.

Thinly slice the other piece of the coconut with a sharp knife, mandoline, or vegetable peeler. Toast the slices in the oven at 300°F (150°C) until light reddish.

Just before serving, fluff the rice with a fork and add the coconut slices and currants.

Lemon Rice with Cashews

Unlike the traditional lemon rice rich with South Indian spices and nuts, this recipe is boldly about the freshness of lemon. Use sweet organic lemons, such as Meyer lemons, for best results. This rice pairs well with spicy or fried vegetables and savories.

{SERVES 4}

Boil the water in a small pot.

Sort, wash, and drain the rice according to the instructions on page 67. Set the rice aside.

Wash the lemon half with warm water. Cut it in half lengthwise and slice the halves thinly. Set the lemon aside.

Heat the ghee or oil in a medium pan or pot over moderate heat. When it's hot but not smoking, add the cashew nuts. Fry them until they are light golden. Remove them with a slotted spoon and set them aside.

Add the hing powder to the residue of ghee or oil that is left in the same pan or pot in which you fried the cashews. After a few seconds, add the rice and fry it for 1 to 2 minutes until it turns partially transparent and white. Add the boiling water, turmeric, sliced lemons, and salt. Reduce the heat to minimum, cover, and simmer for 15 to 20 minutes, undisturbed.

In the meantime, dry roast the fenugreek seeds in a skillet or pan over moderately low heat, tossing and turning the spices with a spatula for 5 to 6 minutes until they are a few shades darker and aromatic. Take care not to burn them or they will become bitter! Remove the seeds from the heat, allow them to cool, and grind them into a fine powder.

When the rice is cooked, fold in the cashew nuts and fenugreek powder and garnish it with chopped cilantro.

1½ cups (375 ml) water
1 cup (250 ml) basmati rice
Half of 1 organic lemon
3 Tbsp ghee (page 25) or oil
½ cup (125 ml) cashew nuts
Pinch of hing powder
¼ tsp turmeric powder
1 tsp sea salt, or to taste
2 tsp fenugreek seeds
Handful (20 g) of chopped cilantro, to garnish

Green Mung Dal with Fennel

*High in dietary fiber and nutritious, whole mung dal make a charmingly simple alternative
to hulled, yellow beans. They are available in most supermarkets,
cook almost as fast as skinless split dal, and are easy to digest by all body constitutions.*

{SERVES 4}

1 cup (250 ml) whole mung
    dal (with skins)
8 cups (2 liters) water
Dab of ghee (page 25),
    butter, or oil
½ tsp turmeric powder
2–3 tomatoes
150 g spinach or other leafy
    greens
¼ tsp cayenne pepper
1 tsp organic whole cane
    sugar
2 Tbsp crème fraîche
    (page 33) or cream
2–3 tsp sea salt, or to taste

FOR THE TEMPERING
1–2 Tbsp ghee
1 tsp fennel seeds, lightly
    crushed
½ tsp jeera seeds
1 green chili, split
1 tsp methi (dry fenugreek
    leaves)
¼ tsp hing powder

TO SERVE
2 Tbsp lemon juice

Sort, wash, and drain the dal. Set it aside.

Bring the water to a boil in a medium to large pot over high heat. When it is boiling, reduce the heat to moderate and add the dal. As soon as a layer of foam appears on the top, remove the foam and add a dab of ghee, butter, or oil, and turmeric. Cover the pot and cook the mixture for 20 minutes, occasionally stirring. You may want to keep the lid ajar at first because the dal tends to boil over.

In the meantime, wash, peel, and remove the stems of the tomatoes. Quarter them and set them aside.

Wash and blanch the spinach. Chop it roughly.

When the dal has cooked for 20 minutes, add the tomatoes. Cover and cook the mixture for 10 minutes then add the spinach. Cover and cook the mixture again for 5 to 7 minutes until the dal and tomatoes are very soft. Mix the dal every 4 or 5 minutes while cooking. Then, reduce the heat to minimum.

Add the cayenne, sugar, crème fraîche or cream, and salt.

Make the tempering by heating up the ghee or oil in a small pan or pot over moderate heat. When it's hot but not smoking, add the crushed fennel seeds and jeera. Fry the spices for about 30 seconds until they turn a few shades darker and aromatic. Add the chili and dry fenugreek leaves. Toss and turn the spices with a spatula a couple of times, and add the hing powder. Pour the tempering into the dal.

Turn off the heat and let the flavors steep for at least 5 minutes. Before serving, pour the lemon juice over the dal.

Jagannath Dal

In the town of Puri, Eastern Indian state of Odisha, channa dal is served at the twelfth-century temple of Sri Jagannath, the Lord of the universe, as one of the offerings prepared six times a day by over five hundred cooks. Known as mahaprashad *(great mercy), the remnants are distributed to hundreds of thousands of visitors. The original recipe of the temple kitchen appears to be a well-guarded secret. My robust offering for the pleasure of Sri Jagannath follows the traditional ingredients but is cooked slightly differently to retain the yellow color.*

{SERVES 4}

Sort, wash, and soak the dal for at least 8 hours or overnight. Drain and set it aside.

Bring the water to a boil in a large pot over high heat. When it is boiling, reduce the heat to moderate and add the dal. As soon as a layer of foam appears on the top, remove the foam and add a dab of ghee, butter, or oil. Also add the turmeric powder, cinnamon stick, cloves, cardamom pods, and tej patta. Cover the pot and cook the dal for 45 to 60 minutes, stirring every 5 to 7 minutes. You may want to keep the lid ajar at first because the dal tends to boil over.

Dry roast the jeera and coriander seeds in a skillet or pan over moderate to moderately low heat for 5 to 6 minutes until they turn a few shades darker. Let it cool and grind the mixture into powder.

Add the powdered spices, coconut, sugar and salt, into the dal when it's cooked. Reduce the heat to minimum and cover again.

Heat the ghee over moderate heat until it is hot but not smoking. Add the panch phoron. As soon as the mustard seeds in the spice mix turn gray and pop, add the black pepper and hing powder. Pour the tempering into the dal. Turn off the heat and let the flavors steep for at least 5 minutes.

Garnish the dal with fresh cilantro before serving.

1 cup (250 ml) channa dal
8 cups (2 liters) water
Dab of ghee (page 25), butter, or oil
½ tsp turmeric
2" (5 cm) piece of cinnamon or cassia bark
4 whole cloves
4 green cardamom pods
1 tej patta
1 tsp jeera seeds
1 tsp coriander seeds
3 Tbsp fresh or desiccated coconut
2 tsp organic whole cane sugar or jaggery
1–2 tsp sea salt, or to taste

FOR THE TEMPERING
1–2 Tbsp ghee or oil
1 tsp panch phoron (page 57)
½ tsp freshly ground black pepper
¼ tsp hing powder

TO SERVE
Handful (20 g) of fresh cilantro

Green Mango Dal

Raw, green mango is pleasantly tart and can be used in any stage of unripeness.
The less ripe the fruit is, the more sour the taste will be. Balance the amount of sugar accordingly.

You can make this dal using toor dal as well. Soak it for an hour or two before boiling it.
The cooking time will be twice as long as with yellow split mung dal.

{SERVES 4}

½ cup (125 ml) yellow split
   mung dal
6 cups (1.5 liters) water
Dab of ghee (page 25),
   butter, or oil
½ tsp turmeric powder
2–3 (450 g) green, unripe
   mangoes
1–2 tomatoes
2 Tbsp fresh cilantro,
   chopped

FOR THE TEMPERING
1–2 Tbsp ghee or oil
½ tsp black mustard seeds
1 tsp jeera seeds
10 small curry leaves (fresh)
¼ tsp hing powder
1 Tbsp fresh, finely grated
   ginger
1–2 green chilies, slit

TO SERVE
3 Tbsp fresh, grated coconut
1 Tbsp sugar, or to taste
2½ tsp sea salt, or to taste

Sort, wash, and drain the dal. Set it aside.

Bring the water to a boil in a medium pot over high heat. When it is boiling, reduce the heat to moderate and add the dal. As it comes to boil, a layer of foam may appear on the top. Remove it and add a dab of ghee, butter, or oil, and turmeric. Cover the pot partially.

Wash, peel, core, and dice the mangoes into ⅔-inch (1.5 cm) cubes. Set the fruit aside.

Wash, peel, and remove the stem from the tomatoes. Chop them and set them aside.

When the dal has cooked for 20 minutes, whisk it and add the mango and tomato chunks and the cilantro. Cook the mixture for 6 to 8 minutes until the mangoes are tender. Reduce the heat to minimum.

Heat the ghee or oil in a small saucepan or pot over moderate heat. When it's hot but not smoking, add the mustard seeds. As soon as they turn gray and pop, add the jeera seeds and curry leaves. Fry them, tossing and turning the spices with a spatula for 20 seconds. Then, add the hing powder, immediately followed by the ginger and chilies. Fry them for 1 minute and pour them into the dal.

Add the coconut, sugar, and salt. Turn off the heat, cover the pot again, and let the flavors steep for at least 5 minutes before serving.

Kitchari

(Rice and Dal Porridge)

Kitchari (or khichdi or kitchuri) has been my favorite breakfast item for the past twenty-five years. What a balanced and nutritious way to start a day! In translation, the word "porridge" is a disservice for such a dish in which protein, grain, and vegetables all flourish together. The recipe is flexible and easy to modify according to what ingredients are available in addition to tomatoes.

{SERVES 4}

Sort, wash, and drain the mung dal. Set it aside.

Bring the water to a boil in a medium to large pot over high heat. When it is boiling, reduce the heat to moderate and add the dal. As soon as a layer of foam appears on the top, remove it and add a dab of ghee, butter, or oil, and turmeric. Cover the pot and cook for 20 minutes, occasionally stirring. You may want to keep the lid ajar at first because the dal tends to boil over.

In the meantime, wash and peel the tomatoes, remove the stems, and cut them into wedges. Set the tomatoes aside.

Sort, wash, and drain the rice.

When the dal has cooked for about 20 minutes, add the tomatoes, rice, and salt. Reduce the heat to minimum, cover the pot, and simmer the ingredients for 10 to 15 minutes.

Heat the ghee or oil in a small pot or pan over moderate heat. When it's hot but not smoking, add the panch phoron. When the mustard seeds turn gray and pop, add the black pepper and hing powder, immediately followed by the ginger and chili. Toss and turn the pan for 30 seconds and pour the spices into the kitchari. Let the flavors steep for at least 5 minutes before serving.

Add the yogurt and the chopped cilantro. Serve the kitchari with lemon wedges and a generous sprinkle of extra virgin olive oil or ghee.

½ cup (125 ml) yellow split mung dal
5 cups (1.25 liters) water
Dab of ghee (page 25), butter, or oil
½ tsp turmeric powder
3 tomatoes
¾ cup (188 ml) basmati rice
1½ tsp sea salt, or to taste

FOR THE TEMPERING
1–2 Tbsp ghee or oil
1 tsp panch phoron (page 57)
½ tsp freshly ground black pepper
¼ tsp hing powder
1 Tbsp fresh, finely grated ginger
1 green chili, slit

TO SERVE
1 cup (250 ml) yogurt
Handful (20 g) of fresh cilantro
Lemon wedges
Extra virgin olive oil

Quinoa Kitchari

*Naturally gluten-free quinoa is sometimes referred as a superfood due to the high protein content
and the presence of essential amino acids, calcium, phosphorus, and iron. It's an alternative to rice
and makes an excellent kitchari. Feel free to use any combination of spinach, potatoes, cauliflower,
carrots, broccoli, zucchini . . . Really, the sky is the limit! Remember to consider their cooking time
when chopping the vegetables; leave bigger those that cook faster than the slow-cooking ones.*

{SERVES 4}

⅓ cup (83 ml) yellow split
  mung dal
6 cups (1.5 liters) water,
  divided
Dab of ghee (page 25),
  butter, or oil
½ tsp turmeric powder
1 cup (250 ml) quinoa
½ tsp sea salt, or to taste
4 cups (1 liter) mixed vegetables, chopped

FOR THE TEMPERING
1–2 Tbsp ghee or oil
1 Tbsp finely grated ginger
  (juice removed)
1 tej patta
¼ tsp freshly ground black
  pepper
¼ tsp hing powder
1½ tsp sea salt, or to taste

TO SERVE
1 Tbsp coriander seeds
Handful (20 g) of fresh herbs,
  chopped
Lemon wedges
Extra virgin olive oil

Sort, wash, and drain the mung dal. Set it aside. Bring 4 cups
(1 liter) of the water to a boil in a medium to large pot over high
heat. When it is boiling, reduce the heat to moderate and add the
dal. As soon as a layer of foam appears on the top, remove it and
add a dab of ghee, butter, or oil, and turmeric. Cover the pot and
cook the dal for 20 minutes, occasionally stirring. You may want to
keep the lid ajar at first because the dal tends to boil over.

Sort, wash, and drain the quinoa. Bring the remaining 2 cups
(500 ml) of the water and salt to boil in a separate pot over high
heat. Add the quinoa, reduce the heat to moderately low, and simmer, covered, for 20 to 30 minutes until the water is absorbed and
the quinoa is light and fluffy. Turn off the heat.

Meanwhile, wash and cut the vegetables into bite-size pieces. Set
them aside.

Heat the ghee or oil in a third pan or pot over moderate heat.
When it's hot but not smoking, add the ginger (juice removed) and
tej patta. Fry the ginger until it becomes light golden, then add the
black pepper and hing, immediately followed by the vegetables.
Sauté the vegetables for a couple minutes and add the cooked dal
with the cooking water. Add the salt. Reduce the heat to moderately low and simmer, covered, for 6 to 10 minutes until the vegetables are tender but not mushy.

Grind the coriander seeds into powder. When the vegetables are
cooked, add the powder with the cooked quinoa into the kitchari.
Turn off the heat and let the flavors steep for at least 5 minutes.

Garnish the kitchari with fresh herbs and serve it with lemon
wedges and extra virgin olive oil.

QUINOA
KHICHDI

Eggplant Lentil Sambar with Curry Leaves

Sambar represents the ancient tradition of lentil-based vegetable stews of South India. It's made with pigeon peas (toor dal), tamarind paste, and sambar masala. Curry leaves play an essential role in it, too. You can use beans, okra, carrots, pumpkin, potatoes, and many other seasonal vegetables either instead of or combined with eggplant. Together with rice, sambar provides a healthy, protein-filled meal.

{SERVES 4}

Sort, wash, and drain the dal. Set aside.

Bring the water to a boil in a medium to large pot over high heat. Start cooking with 4 cups (1 liter) of water for a thicker sambar, and with 6 cups (1.5 liters) water if you like a thinner sambar.

When the water is boiling, reduce the heat to moderate and add the dal. As soon as a layer of foam appears on the top, remove it and add a dab of ghee, butter, or oil, and turmeric. Cover the pot and cook the dal for 30 minutes, occasionally stirring. You may want to keep the lid ajar at first because the dal tends to boil over.

Meanwhile, wash and crack open the coconut. Remove the thin, brown skin. Place the coconut and boiling water in a blender and process the fruit until it turns into a white paste. Strain it and set the liquid aside. Save the leftover pulp for cooking or baking.

Wash and cut the eggplant into small cubes. Set them aside.

Wash, peel, and remove the stems from the tomatoes. Cut them into wedges and set them aside.

When the dal has cooked for 30 to 40 minutes and is soft, add the eggplant dices. Cook for 5 to 6 minutes, then add the tomatoes, cayenne, sambar powder, tamarind concentrate, sugar, salt, and coconut milk. Reduce the heat to moderately low and cook, covered, until the vegetables are soft, for about 10 minutes. Mix it every 4 or 5 minutes while cooking.

Make the tempering by heating up the ghee or oil in a small pot or pan over moderate heat. When it's hot but not smoking, add the mustard seeds. As soon as they turn gray and pop, add the curry leaves, hing powder, and black pepper. Toss and turn the spices with a spatula once and pour the tempering into the sambar. Mix the ingredients well and let the flavors steep for at least 5 minutes before serving. Garnish with fresh cilantro.

½ cup (125 ml) toor dal
4–6 cups (1–1.5 liters) water
Dab of ghee (page 25), butter, or oil
½ tsp turmeric
1 coconut
2 cups (500 ml) boiling water
1 eggplant
2–3 tomatoes
½ tsp cayenne powder
1 Tbsp sambar powder (page 54)
1 tsp tamarind concentrate
½ Tbsp organic whole cane sugar
2½ tsp sea salt, or to taste

FOR THE TEMPERING
1–2 Tbsp ghee or oil
¾ tsp black mustard seeds
10–15 fresh, small curry leaves
¼ tsp hing powder
¼ tsp freshly ground black pepper

TO SERVE
Handful (20 g) of fresh cilantro, chopped

Upma

I hesitated to include upma in the book because, being a savory porridge similar to kitchari, it looks and sounds somewhat plain. However, we love it at home and consider it one of the most comforting breakfast dishes. It's quick to make if you steam the vegetables, boil the water, and roast the semolina simultaneously on three separate burners. Cauliflower, carrots, and peas are common vegetables in upma, but you may also use green beans, peppers, Brussels sprouts, or cabbage.

{SERVES 4}

4 cups (1 liter) chopped
  vegetables
4–5½ cups (1.5 liters) water,
  divided
2¼ tsp sea salt, divided
2 Tbsp ghee (page 25)
  or butter
1 cup (250 ml) fine,
  wholegrain semolina
  (spelt or wheat)

FOR THE TEMPERING
1–2 Tbsp ghee or oil
¾ tsp black mustard seeds
½ tsp jeera seeds
10–15 small, fresh curry leaves
1 tsp freshly ground black
  pepper
½ tsp hing powder
½ tsp turmeric powder
1 Tbsp finely grated, fresh
  ginger
1 green chili, slit
2 tomatoes, peeled and chopped

TO SERVE
1 Tbsp coriander seeds

In a covered pot, steam the vegetables in ½ cup (125 ml) of water and ¼ teaspoon salt for 7 to 9 minutes over moderate heat until they are soft. By the time they are ready, the water should have been absorbed and evaporated.

At the same time, bring the rest of the water and 2 teaspoons salt to a boil in another, covered pot over high heat. As soon as it boils, turn off the heat. Adjust the amount of water according to the consistency you want to achieve. For a wet, soft upma, use 5 cups (1.25 liters) water.

Melt 2 tablespoons ghee or butter in a heavy-bottomed pan or pot over moderate heat. Add the semolina and cook it for 10 to 15 minutes, constantly stirring, until it turns a few shades darker and aromatic. Then, add the boiling water gradually while whisking the semolina. It will sputter, be careful! When the water has incorporated evenly, turn off the heat and add the steamed vegetables.

Heat the ghee or oil in a small pan over moderate heat. When it's hot but not smoking, add the mustard seeds. As soon as they turn gray and pop, add the jeera seeds and curry leaves. Fry them for a couple of seconds, then add the black pepper, hing, and turmeric, immediately followed by the ginger and chili. Fry for 1 minute and, finally, add the chopped tomatoes. Cook the mixture for 4 to 5 minutes until the tomatoes are soft. Pour the tempering into the upma, mix well, and cover.

Grind and add the coriander seeds into the upma before serving.

VEGETABLE DISHES

Spiced Green Beans / 88

Cabbage and Kale
with Ground Poppy Seeds / 91

Bitter Melon Crisps / 92

Spiced Okra / 95

Brussels Sprouts
in Savory Cream / 96

Beet Kofta
in Sour Cream Sauce / 99

Cabbage Kofta / 103

Root Vegetable Frites / 107

Cauliflower Coconut Curry with
Peas and Fried Cheese / 108

Green Bean Tomato Curry
with Fried Cheese Balls / 111

Palak Paneer (Spinach
and Fresh Cheese) / 112

Baby Potatoes in
Yogurt-Tomato Sauce / 115

Potato Curry from Mathura / 116

Peas with Paneer and Cilantro / 119

Roasted Vegetables / 120

Pumpkin and Spinach Curry / 123

Carrot and Pumpkin Soup / 124

Bengali-Style Vegetables
with Ground Mustard Seed / 126

Spiced Green Beans

This quick side dish exudes true character. You may try it with any kind of beans available or in season.
If you prefer a milder taste, substitute a portion of beans with potatoes cut into bean-size sticks.
Use full-fat homemade yogurt in this recipe because it tolerates cooking better than
store-bought yogurt, which has a tendency to curdle and split. Remember to whisk the yogurt,
add it at room temperature, and stir it while it boils.

{SERVES 4}

4 cups (1 liter) green beans
½ cup (125 ml) water for
   steaming
1 Tbsp coriander seeds
½–1 tsp cayenne powder
2 tsp amchoor powder
¼ tsp sugar
2 tsp sea salt, or to taste
½ cup (125 ml) homemade
   yogurt, at room temperature

FOR THE TEMPERING
2–3 Tbsp ghee (page 25) or oil
½ tsp kalonji seeds
½ tsp turmeric powder
¼ tsp hing powder
2 green chilies, slit

Wash and trim the beans into shorter, bite-size pieces.

Bring the water to a boil in a pot over high heat. Add the beans and reduce the heat to moderate. Steam them, covered, for 4 to 5 minutes. Then remove the pot from the heat, strain the beans, and plunge them in cold water to stop the cooking. Drain the beans again and set them aside.

Dry roast the coriander seeds on a pan or skillet over a moderate to moderately low heat for 5 to 6 minutes until they turn a few shades darker and become aromatic. Remove the seeds, let them cool, and grind them into powder.

Whisk the spices, sugar, salt, and yogurt together in a small bowl. Set the mixture aside.

Heat the ghee or oil in a pan or wok over moderate heat. When it's hot but not smoking, add the kalonji seeds and, 30 seconds later, the turmeric, hing, and chilies. Toss and turn the spices with a spatula once and add the beans. Mix the green beans to coat them with the spices and fry for 2 minutes, stirring constantly.

Add the yogurt mixture and reduce the heat to low. Cook, stirring for 3 to 4 minutes. Remove the beans from the heat and serve as soon as possible.

Cabbage and Kale
with Ground Poppy Seeds

Every year fresh, green cabbage is one of the first spring vegetables to hit the market.
Unlike old cabbage stored over the winter, spring cabbage is lush and mellow. It pairs very well with kale.
The addition of poppy seed and mustard sauce gives this dish its strong taste. Start with a smaller
amount of mustard seeds and increase the amount according to your taste. Always grind the seeds in
a mortar to avoid bitterness, and add them at the end of cooking.

{SERVES 4}

Mix the boiling water, poppy, and mustard seeds in a bowl. Set it aside.

Heat the ghee or oil over moderate heat. When it is hot but not smoking, add the kalonji seeds, black pepper, and hing, immediately followed by the cabbage and kale. Fry the vegetables for a few minutes, add the butter, and reduce the heat to moderately low. Cook the mixture uncovered until the cabbage is soft. Mix occasionally. If there is any liquid on the bottom, increase the heat to medium until it has evaporated.

Meanwhile, finely grate the coconut, if using. Add it with the sugar and salt to the cooked cabbage and kale. Turn off the heat.

Grind the poppy and mustard seed water into a fine paste. Mix it with the cabbage. Serve immediately.

½ cup (125 ml) boiling water
4 Tbsp white poppy seeds
½–1 tsp black mustard seeds
1–2 Tbsp ghee (page 25) or oil
1 tsp kalonji seeds
¾ tsp freshly ground black pepper
¼ tsp hing powder
6 cups (1.5 liters) shredded young, green cabbage
5 cups (1.25 liters) shredded kale
¼ cup (60 g) butter
Half of 1 fresh coconut half (optional)
½ Tbsp sugar
¾ tsp sea salt, or to taste

Bitter Melon Crisps

Pleasantly bitter, these crispy chips are excellent appetizers, usually served at the beginning of a meal. They activate digestive juices and add a surprising savory element to the palate.

Bitter melon is sometimes called bitter gourd or bitter squash. You will find it in Asian grocery stores by the name karela or kantola. It is a dark green vegetable with warty exterior and oblong shape. Different from the Chinese cultivar, which is twice or three times the size, karela is only 2 to 4 inches (5 to 10 cm) long.

Karela contains the phytonutrient polypeptide-P, a plant insulin also found in fenugreek seeds, wild blueberries, and ginseng. In addition, it composes a hypoglycemic agent called charantin, which increases glucose uptake and glycogen synthesis in the cells of liver, muscle, and adipose tissue. These natural compounds reduce blood sugar levels. Bitter melon pods are rich in vitamins A, B, and C, as well as in minerals such as iron, zinc, potassium, manganese, and magnesium.

If you are pregnant or breast-feeding, avoid karela because the bitter taste may cause the stomach and womb to pulsate. Babies and small children may be sensitive to vicine found in the seeds of karela.

{SERVES 4}

2 cups (500 ml) thinly sliced
   bitter melon (karela)
1 Tbsp ghee (page 25) or oil
5 Tbsp rice flour
2 Tbsp corn flour
1½ tsp cayenne powder
¼ tsp turmeric (optional)
½ tsp sea salt, or to taste

Preheat the oven to 425°F (220°C).

Mix the bitter melon slices with ghee or oil in a bowl.

Whisk the flours, spices, and salt in a separate bowl. Dip the slices, one by one, into the flour, coat each slice evenly, and place the slices in a single layer on a baking sheet.

Bake 15 to 20 minutes until the bitter melons are crisp and golden. If need be, turn them once or twice while baking.

Spiced Okra

Okra is a lovely vegetable as long as it's properly prepared. Usually shallow-fried, oven baking also gives a good result. Remember to thoroughly dry the pods after washing them. Use only a clean, dry knife and utensils to minimize okra's tendency to become sticky and gooey.

{SERVES 4}

Wash and dry the okra with a cloth or paper towel. Cut off the stems and slit the pods lengthwise in quarters.

Combine the spices, chickpea flour, and okra in a bowl.

Heat as much ghee or oil as needed for shallow frying over moderately high heat. Add a handful of okra at a time and fry it until it's golden on all sides. Remove it with a slotted spoon. Repeat and fry the okra in batches. You may need to add ghee or oil as you go.

Alternatively, rub a couple of tablespoons of ghee or oil with your hands into the okra after washing and drying it. Then, mix the vegetable pieces with the spices, salt, and chickpea flour. Place the okra on an oven tray on a single layer and bake it at 425°F (220°C) until the slices are fork-tender and golden.

Before serving, sprinkle the slices liberally with chaat masala.

5 cups (1.25 liters) okra
1 tsp cayenne powder
1 tsp turmeric powder
½ tsp amchoor powder
½ tsp garam masala (page 58)
1 tsp sea salt, or to taste
6 Tbsp chickpea flour (besan)
Ghee (page 25) or oil as needed

TO SERVE
Chaat masala (page 61),
 to garnish

Brussels Sprouts in Savory Cream

Instead of Brussels sprouts, you can make this dish with many other vegetables, such as broccoli, zucchini, eggplant, cauliflower, or even cabbage, but without steaming them first. If you sauté the vegetables directly in the hot ghee or oil after briefly frying the black pepper, hing, and curry powder, you will have to simmer them for a longer time in cream until the vegetables are fully cooked.

Or, you can roast the vegetables in the oven, and then drop them into the hot ghee or oil after briefly frying the black pepper, hing, and curry powder in it. Then, add the cream, kala namak powder, and salt, and bring the cream to a boil.

You can also combine all the ingredients (except water) in an ovenproof dish and cook them at 425 °F (220 °C) as long as it takes for the vegetables to become tender.

By changing the method of cooking, the outcome will be different, although the components of the dish remain the same.

{SERVES 4}

1¾ lbs (800 g) Brussels
  sprouts
½ cup (125 ml) water
1–2 Tbsp ghee (page 25),
  butter, or oil
½ tsp freshly ground black
  pepper
¼ tsp hing powder
1 tsp curry powder
¼ cup (63 ml) cream
½ tsp kala namak powder
½ tsp sea salt, or to taste

Wash the Brussels sprouts and remove the stems. Steam them in the water for 8 to 10 minutes until they are fork tender. Plunge them in cold water to stop cooking, then drain them.

Heat the ghee, butter, or oil in a pan or wok over moderate heat. When it's hot but not smoking, add the black pepper, hing, and curry powder. Toss and turn the spices with a spatula once, and add the Brussels sprouts, cream, kala namak, and salt. Reduce the heat to minimum and simmer, uncovered, for 5 minutes or until the Brussels sprouts are fully cooked.

Beet Kofta in Sour Cream Sauce

Entertaining and surprising, these koftas are an eye-catcher! When I ran a catering service, they were one of the most wanted menu items. They present such a nice balance of sweetness and saltiness, and they look stunning. My clients called them love dumplings!

{MAKES 25–30 BALLS}

3 cups (750 ml) finely grated
  beets
1½ tsp freshly ground black
  pepper
Generous pinch hing powder
Generous pinch cardamom
  powder
Generous pinch clove powder
¼ tsp cinnamon powder
3 Tbsp sesame seeds
3 Tbsp desiccated coconut
1¼ tsp sea salt, or to taste
2 tsp baking powder
½–1 cup (125–250 ml) chickpea
  flour (besan), as needed
Ghee (page 25) or oil,
  for deep frying

FOR THE SOUR CREAM
SAUCE
3 cups (750 ml) homemade sour
  cream (page 26), at room
  temperature
1 Tbsp extra virgin olive oil
1 tsp freshly ground black
  pepper
1 tsp sea salt, or to taste
1–3 Tbsp beet juice, for coloring
  the sauce

Strain any excess juice from the grated beets.

Mix the beets, spices, sesame seeds, coconut, salt, and baking powder. Add the chickpea flour gradually. Adjust the amount of flour according to the wetness of the beets. The general rule is to use as little flour as it takes to bind the ingredients together. Too much flour will yield dry and hard koftas. Newly harvested beets call for more flour than winter beets.

/ Continued /

When you are ready to fry the koftas, heat the ghee or oil in a wok or pan over moderate heat. There should be at least 2 inches (5 cm) of ghee or oil on the bottom of the pan, and one-third of the pot should be empty. When you slip the koftas into the wok, the ghee or oil will bubble and sputter. The empty space prevents an overflow.

The ghee or oil is ready when it is hot but not smoking. To test the temperature, drop a small piece of beet into the wok. It should immediately spring to the top and sizzle.

While the ghee or oil is heating up, roll the beet mixture into walnut-size balls between your palms. Place them on a tray or platter.

Slide the balls carefully, one by one, into the hot ghee or oil. The safest way is to use a metal spoon instead of your hands. However, you have to be quick and gently shake them off the spoon because they may get stuck as soon as they come in contact with heat. Avoid overcrowding the pan. Fry the koftas in two or three batches depending on the size of the wok.

It takes about 3 to 5 minutes to thoroughly cook the koftas. Gently move them with a slotted spoon for an even result. They should be light, float on the top, and turn some shades darker. If the temperature drops too much, the koftas will be soggy. If it rises too high, they will burn on the outside but remain uncooked in the center. Try to keep the temperature steady and moderate.

When the koftas are ready, lift them with a slotted spoon, and drain them in a sieve, colander, or paper towels. When you have fried all of them, make the sauce.

Whisk the sour cream, olive oil, black pepper, salt, and beet juice together in a bowl. Add the juice gradually to achieve the shade of pink you like.

Cover the koftas with the sauce. Serve them at room temperature or, if you want to serve them warm, place the bowl, covered, in the gently heated oven for 10 to 15 minutes. Remember that the sour cream will curdle if it passes the boiling point.

Note: Wearing vinyl gloves will keep your hands clean while working with beets.

Cabbage Kofta

Cabbage koftas are easy to make even in large quantities. This recipe is mild and serves everyone from a toddler to the elderly with sensitive palates. For a spicier dish, add finely grated ginger and one or two green chilies. If cabbage isn't to your liking substitute zucchini, cauliflower, or mixed vegetables. Easily absorbing liquid and flavor, koftas are served in tomato, yogurt, or cream sauce. Plain, they can be eaten as snacks.

{MAKES 25–30 BALLS}

Dry roast the coriander and jeera seeds in a skillet or pan over moderate to moderately low heat, tossing and turning the spices with a spatula for 5 to 6 minutes until they become a few shades darker and aromatic. Remove the pan from the heat and let the spices cool. Grind them into powder.

Remove any liquid the cabbage might have released. Mix the cabbage, coriander-jeera powder, black pepper, turmeric, coconut, sesame, salt, cilantro, and baking powder. Add the chickpea flour gradually. Adjust the amount of flour according to the wetness of the cabbage. The general rule is to use only as little flour as it takes to bind the ingredients together. Too much flour will yield dry and hard koftas. Newly harvested, green cabbage calls for more flour than winter cabbage.

When you are ready to fry the koftas, heat the ghee or oil in a wok or pan over moderate heat. There should be at least 2 inches (5 cm) of ghee or oil on the bottom of the pan, and one-third of the pot should be empty. When you slip the koftas into the wok, the ghee or oil will bubble and sputter. The empty space prevents an overflow.

Ghee or oil is ready when it is hot but not smoking. To test the temperature, drop a small piece of cabbage into the wok. It should immediately spring to the top and sizzle.

While the ghee or oil is heating up, roll the cabbage mixture into tight, walnut-size balls between your palms. Place them on a tray or platter.

1½ tsp coriander seeds

1½ tsp jeera seeds

4–5 cups (1–1.25 liters) finely grated cabbage

½ tsp freshly ground black pepper

¼ tsp turmeric powder

3 Tbsp desiccated coconut

3 Tbsp sesame seeds

1½ tsp sea salt, or to taste

2 handfuls (40 g) of fresh cilantro, chopped

2 tsp baking powder

½–1 cup (125–250 ml) chickpea flour (besan), as needed

Ghee (page 25) or oil, for deep frying

/ Continued /

Slide the balls carefully, one by one, into the hot ghee or oil. The safest way is to use a metal spoon instead of your hands. However, you have to be quick and softly shake them off the spoon because they may get stuck as soon as they come in contact with heat. Avoid overcrowding the pan. Fry the koftas in two or three batches depending on the size of the wok.

It takes 3 to 5 minutes to thoroughly cook the koftas. Gently move them with a slotted spoon for an even result. They should be light, float on the top, and turn several shades darker. If the temperature drops too much, the koftas will be soggy. If it rises too high, they will burn externally but remain uncooked in the center. Try to keep the temperature steady and moderate.

When the koftas are ready, lift them with a slotted spoon and drain them in a sieve, colander, or paper towels. When you have fried all of them, make the tomato sauce according to the recipe on page 192.

Root Vegetable Frites

Baked celeriac (celery root) is an excellent side dish or snack.
Enjoy it with your pick of chutney. For color and diversity, mix celeriac with
other root vegetables, such as beets, carrots, parsnips, and turnips.

{SERVES 4}

Preheat the oven to 425°F (220°C).

Wash, peel, and cut the celeriac into ½-inch (125 mm) sticks.

Combine all the ingredients in a large bowl and mix them thoroughly. Place the celeriac sticks on a baking sheet in a single layer.

Bake 20 to 30 minutes, occasionally tossing the celeriac, until it is tender and golden.

42 oz (1.2 kg) celeriac
1–2 Tbsp ghee (page 25) or oil
¼ tsp hing powder
½ tsp freshly ground black pepper
½ tsp sweet paprika powder
Pinch of smoked paprika powder
¼ tsp cayenne powder
1 tsp sea salt, or to taste

Cauliflower Coconut Curry
with Peas and Fresh Cheese

In this mild curry, the cauliflower simmers in a coconut-based broth.
You can use either plain or fried paneer. Both are equally delicious.
Try substituting cauliflower and peas with other seasonal vegetables for a different flavor.

{SERVES 4}

12 oz (335 g) paneer, pressed, diced, and plain, or fried (page 42)

1 cup (250 ml) freshly grated coconut

2 tomatoes

21 oz (600 g) cauliflower

1 cup (250 ml) green peas, fresh or frozen

1–2 Tbsp ghee (page 25) or oil

2 tsp shredded ginger (juice removed)

1 tej patta

1 green chili, slit

½ tsp jeera seeds

½ tsp freshly ground black pepper

¼ tsp hing powder

1½ cup (375 ml) water or whey

½ tsp turmeric powder

2 tsp sea salt, or to taste

TO SERVE

½ tsp garam masala (page 58)

Handful (20 g) of fresh mint or cilantro, chopped

Make the cheese from 12 cups (3 liters) of milk according to the instructions on page 42.

Peel off and discard the brown skin from the coconut. Scrape or grate the white meat and set aside. Wash, peel, or blanch the tomatoes and remove the stems. Place them in a food processor with the grated coconut. Process until there is a smooth paste. Set the paste aside.

Wash and cut the cauliflower into florets. Set it aside.

Wash and remove the peas from the pods, if you are using fresh peas. Take the frozen peas out of the freezer, if you are using them. Set the peas aside.

Heat the ghee or oil in a pan or wok over moderate heat. When it is hot but not smoking, add the ginger (juice removed), tej patta, and slit chili. When the ginger turns light golden, add the jeera seeds. Fry them, tossing and turning the spices with a spatula, for 20 to 30 seconds, then add the black pepper and hing powder immediately followed by the tomato and coconut paste. Fry it all, mixing often, for 2 to 3 minutes.

Add the water or whey, turmeric, and salt. Bring the mixture to boil then reduce the heat to moderately low and add the cauliflower. Simmer for 12 minutes. Then, add the fresh green peas and paneer cubes. Simmer for 5 minutes or until the cauliflower is fully cooked. If you are using frozen peas, add them now.

Turn off the heat, remove the tej patta and add the garam masala. Mix and let the flavors steep for at least 5 minutes before serving. Garnish with the chopped mint or cilantro.

Green Bean Tomato Curry
with Fried Cheese Balls

Use any combination of string and French beans that come in green and purple varieties and yellow wax beans. When in season, add baby broad beans, fresh chickpeas, or green peas. You can also use bell peppers, broccoli, cauliflower, eggplant, humble potato, or any other vegetable in the tomato sauce instead. Regardless, fried cheese balls will steal the show! Remember, different vegetables have various cooking times.

{SERVES 4}

Make the fried cheese balls as instructed on page 45.

Wash, peel, or blanch the tomatoes, and press them through a sieve. Discard the seeds. Set the puree aside.

Wash, trim, and cut the beans shorter if they are long. Set the beans aside.

Wash and shell the peas. Set the peas aside.

Heat the ghee or oil in a pan or pot over moderate heat. When it's hot but not smoking, add the mustard seeds. As soon as they turn gray and pop, add the urad dal. When the urad dal turn light golden, add the curry leaves, turmeric, hing, ginger, and chopped chilies. Fry for 1 minute, then add the tomato paste.

Cover the pot and cook for 10 to 15 minutes, occasionally stirring, until the tomato paste separates from the oil. Add 1 cup (250 ml) water or whey. As soon as it starts to boil, add the beans. Cook for 7 to 10 minutes until the beans are tender but not overcooked. Reduce the heat to minimum.

Add the peas, cream, garam masala, sugar, salt, and cheese balls. You may want to add more water or whey if the dish looks too dry. Simmer for a couple of minutes, turn off the heat, and let the flavors steep for at least 5 minutes before serving. Garnish with fresh cilantro.

1 batch fried cheese balls (page 45)
5 medium-size tomatoes
8 cups (2 liters) mixed green beans and peas in the pod
3–4 Tbsp ghee (page 25) or oil
½ tsp black mustard seeds
1 tsp split urad dal
20 small curry leaves
½ tsp turmeric powder
⅓ tsp hing powder
2 tsp fresh, grated ginger
1–2 green chilies, seeded and chopped
1–1½ cups (250–375 ml) water or whey
2 Tbsp cream
¾ tsp garam masala (page 58)
2 tsp sugar, or to taste
2½ tsp sea salt, or to taste

TO SERVE
Handful (20 g) of fresh cilantro, chopped

Palak Paneer
(Spinach and Fresh Cheese)

*Spinach, along with other leafy greens, is one of my favorite vegetables. In all the unlimited ways
to prepare it, this veggie never fails to taste superb. Palak paneer is a well-known North Indian dish,
popular in restaurant menus. My version is based on just a few simple flavors.
To retain an emerald green hue, cook the spinach as quickly as possible.*

{SERVES 4}

12 oz (335 g) paneer, pressed
and cubed (page 42)
21 oz (600 g) spinach
½ cup (125 ml) water, or as
needed
2 Tbsp fresh, finely grated
ginger
2–3 green chilies, seeded
1 Tbsp fennel seed
1–2 Tbsp ghee (page 25) or oil
½ tsp jeera seeds
¼ tsp freshly ground black
pepper
¼ tsp hing powder
1 tsp sugar
½–1 tsp sea salt, or to taste
⅓ cup (83 ml) heavy cream
or crème fraîche (page 33)
½ tsp kala namak
3 Tbsp lemon juice, or to
taste

Make, press, and dice the paneer from 12 cups (3 liters) of milk
according to the instructions on page 42.

Wash the spinach thoroughly in several changes of water.
Blanch it in a pot of boiling water for 2 minutes. Remove the pot
from the heat, drain the spinach, and refresh it under cold water to
stop the cooking process. Drain again. Use a blender, adding ½ cup
water or as needed to make a smooth puree. Set the puree aside.

In a spice mill or mortar, make a paste from the grated ginger
and seeded chilies. You may need to add a tablespoon of water to
create the right texture. Set the paste aside.

Dry roast the fennel seeds in a skillet or pan over moderate to
moderately low heat, tossing and turning them with a spatula for 5
to 6 minutes until they become a few shades darker and aromatic.
Remove the seeds from the heat and let them cool. Grind them into
powder and set it aside.

Heat the ghee or oil in a wok or pan over moderate temperature. When it's hot but not smoking, add the jeera seeds. Fry
them for 20 to 30 seconds until they turn a few shades darker and
aromatic. Add the black pepper and hing powder, immediately
followed by the ginger-chili paste. Fry for 30 seconds, then add the
spinach puree. Cook the mixture for 3 minutes.

Add the paneer cubes, fennel powder, sugar, salt, and cream.
Reduce the heat to minimum and simmer for 5 minutes. Turn off
the heat.

Finally, add the kala namak powder and lemon juice before
serving.

Baby Potatoes in Yogurt-Tomato Sauce

*Yogurt and tomatoes form a creamy sauce when cooked together. Homemade curd,
being less sour than the store-bought variety, serves the recipe better. Perfect for days
when the rain pours down, this dish can be scooped with your favorite flatbread.*

{SERVES 4}

Wash the potatoes. Sprinkle them with ghee, butter, or oil; cayenne powder; and salt. Roast them in a preheated oven at 425°F (220°C) for 25 to 30 minutes, occasionally tossing them until they are baked and nicely browned.

Meanwhile, wash, peel, or blanch the tomatoes and remove the stems. Puree the tomatoes in the food processor. Set the puree aside.

Dry roast the coriander, fennel, and jeera seeds in a skillet or pan over moderate to moderately low heat for 5 to 6 minutes, tossing and turning the spices with a spatula until they turn a few shades darker and aromatic. Remove the spices from the heat and let them cool. Grind them into powder. Set it aside.

Heat the ghee or oil in a wok or pan over moderate heat. When it is hot but not smoking, add the grated ginger (juice removed) and tej patta. Toss and fry until the ginger turns lightly golden. Add the cinnamon or cassia bark, cardamom pods, and cloves. Toss and fry for 30 seconds and add the black pepper, turmeric, and hing powder. Toss once, then add the tomato paste. Mix well and cook the mixture for 7 to 8 minutes until the oil separates.

Reduce the heat to low and add the ground spices, yogurt, sugar, kala namak, salt, and water or whey. Mix and add the potatoes. Cover and simmer for 15 to 20 minutes until the gravy thickens.

Remove the whole spices before serving.

2¼ lbs (1 kg) baby potatoes
1 Tbsp ghee (page 25),
   butter, or oil
¼ tsp cayenne powder
½ tsp sea salt, or to taste
2–3 (300 g) tomatoes
2 tsp coriander seeds
1 tsp fennel seeds
1 tsp jeera seeds

FOR THE TEMPERING
1–2 Tbsp ghee or oil
2 tsp fresh grated ginger
   (juice removed)
1 tej patta
2" (5 cm) piece of cinnamon
   stick or cassia bark
4 green cardamom pods
2 cloves
½ tsp freshly ground black
   pepper
¼ tsp turmeric powder
¼ tsp hing powder

FOR THE SAUCE
½ cup (125 ml) yogurt
1 tsp sugar
1 tsp kala namak powder
2 tsp sea salt, or to taste
1 cup (250 ml) water or whey

Potato Curry from Mathura

Potato lovers will enjoy this comforting recipe. It's my version of a potato curry from Mathura, one of the holiest places of pilgrimage in India. You can serve this dish any time of the day with a pile of piping hot rice and puri or paratha. I love to add a generous spoonful of homemade organic yogurt with a thick layer of natural cream on the top just before plating.

{SERVES 4}

1¼ lbs (600 g) potatoes
Pinch of salt
2 cups (500 ml) fresh spinach,
  lightly packed

FOR THE TEMPERING
2–3 Tbsp ghee (page 25) or oil
¾ tsp jeera seeds
¼ tsp hing powder
½ tsp turmeric powder
1 tsp finely grated fresh
  ginger
1 green chili, slit
2 cups (500 ml) whey or
  water
1½ tsp amchoor powder
¼ tsp cayenne powder
1½ tsp salt

TO SERVE
½ tsp kala namak powder
½ cup (125 ml) homemade
  organic yogurt (optional)
Handful (20 g) of fresh dill

Wash and boil the potatoes in a pot of salted water until they are tender but not mushy. Drain, peel, and crush them into smaller chunks with your palm. You can lightly break or mash some of the potatoes with a fork.

While the potatoes are cooking, blanch the spinach in a pot of boiling water for 30 seconds. Remove the pot from the heat, drain the spinach, and refresh it under cold water to stop the cooking process. Drain again, then chop it and set aside.

When the potatoes are ready, heat the ghee or oil in a medium pan or pot over moderate heat. When it's hot but not smoking, add the jeera seeds. Fry them until they become a few shades darker, for 20 to 30 seconds, then add the hing and turmeric powder immediately followed by the ginger and chili. Fry the spices for 1 or 2 minutes, tossing and turning them with a spatula, before adding the potatoes. Coat the potatoes with the spices and add the spinach, whey or water, amchoor, cayenne, and salt. Mix well. Bring the mixture to a boil, reduce the heat to moderately low, and cook for 20 minutes. Stir occasionally. Turn off the heat.

Just before serving, mix in the kala namak powder. Spoon the yogurt on top of each serving, and garnish with fresh dill.

Peas with Paneer and Cilantro

In its simplicity, this dish is the epitome of deliciousness. In each bite, each ingredient and flavor shines. Freshly made, pressed cheese is soft and pillowy. I have minimized the amount of ghee without compromising the caramelized flavor. If you want to use ghee more liberally—and it certainly is not harmful!—add a green chili or a little bit of cayenne powder to counteract the heaviness of dairy.

{SERVES 4}

Make the paneer from 12 cups (3 liters) of milk according to the instructions on the page 42.

Wash and peel the tomatoes and remove the stems. Process them into a paste in a spice mill or blender. Set the paste aside.

If you are using frozen peas, take them out of the freezer now and set them aside in a bowl.

Heat the ghee in a wok or pan over moderate heat. When it's hot but not smoking, add the mustard and jeera seeds. As soon as the mustard seeds turn gray and pop, add the black pepper, curry powder, and hing, immediately followed by the tomato paste. Cover and cook for 10 minutes. Stir occasionally to prevent scorching.

Add the fresh peas, cream, whey, sugar, kala namak, and salt to the tomatoes. Mix well, reduce the heat to low and cook for 5 minutes. Then add the cheese cubes along with the frozen peas, if you are using them instead of fresh ones. Turn off the heat and let the flavors steep for at least 5 minutes before serving.

Garnish with fresh cilantro.

12 oz (335 g) paneer, pressed and diced (page 42)
4–5 (500 g) tomatoes
1 cup (250 ml) green peas, fresh or frozen
2–3 Tbsp ghee (page 25) or oil
1 tsp black mustard seeds
1 tsp jeera seeds
½ tsp freshly ground black pepper
1 tsp curry powder (page 53)
¼ tsp hing powder
½ cup (125 ml) heavy cream
½ cup (125 ml) whey or water
1 tsp organic whole cane sugar
½ tsp kala namak powder
1½–2 tsp sea salt, or to taste

TO SERVE
Handful (20 g) of fresh cilantro

Roasted Vegetables

Roasting is one of the healthiest ways to prepare vegetables. It requires hardly any effort, besides washing and chopping. It is the method to follow when you don't have time to stand in front of the stove but want a solid meal.

When I clean the fridge, I always start by emptying the vegetable drawer on an oven tray. Any leftover bud, stem, shoot, tuber, root, or pod goes! By the time I'm ready, so is my lunch.

Roasting gives a deep, slightly smoky flavor unachievable by any other cooking technique. Try newly harvested, whole fava bean pods for a surprising result, or more conventional vegetables— anything from potatoes to eggplants, pumpkin, or fennel.

Unless you add tomatoes to the mix, roasted vegetables are generally dry. As a side dish, serve them as such; otherwise, fold them in plain yogurt or spicy sour cream sauce.

You can keep the seasoning as simple as salt and pepper, or you may roast the vegetables with curry, sambar, or panch phoron powder, or sprinkle them with garam or chaat masala.

{SERVES 4}

2¼ lbs (1 kg) vegetables
1–2 Tbsp melted ghee (page 25), butter, or oil
½ tsp maple syrup or sugar (optional)
¼ tsp black pepper
⅛–¼ tsp cayenne powder
¼ tsp hing powder
Generous pinch of cinnamon powder or ½ tsp curry powder
1 tsp sea salt, or to taste
Handful (20 g) of fresh herbs (optional)

Preheat the oven to 425°F (220°C).

Wash, peel (if necessary), and chop the vegetables according to your taste. Toss them with the melted ghee, butter, or oil, syrup, spices, salt, and herbs. Transfer the vegetables to a baking sheet in a single layer.

Roast the vegetables in the oven until they are fork tender and golden. Depending on the size and type of vegetables, it takes from 20 to 60 minutes to properly roast them. Insert a skewer or toothpick into the vegetables every now and then; when it goes in effortlessly, the vegetables are ready. You may have to turn the vegetables over once or twice while they are in the oven.

Pumpkin and Spinach Curry

*The simplest method of preparing vegetables is to sauté them in spiced ghee or oil, then simmer
them in their own juices over moderately low temperature. Salt (and turmeric) causes
the vegetables to sweat, or release their juices, so additional liquid is usually not needed.
To make this everyday vegetable dish more festive, add cream or paneer.*

{SERVES 4}

Wash the spinach in several changes of water to remove dust and
sand. Blanch it in a pot of boiling water for 1 minute. Rinse the
spinach with cold water to stop the cooking process, then drain and
chop it coarsely. Set it aside.

Heat the ghee in a medium pan or pot over moderate heat.
When it is hot but not smoking, add the ginger (juice removed)
and tej patta. Fry the ginger until it turns light golden. Add the
panch phoron. Fry it for 30 seconds then add the chili, turmeric,
and hing powder. Toss and turn the spices with a spatula once or
twice and add the pumpkin. Fry for 3 to 4 minutes, occasionally
stirring.

Add the water and salt. Mix well and reduce the heat to moderately low. Cover and simmer the pumpkin for about 10 minutes until it is tender. Stir occasionally and make sure there is always liquid
on the bottom of the pan. Sometimes the vegetables release more
juices than at other times. If at any point the vegetables stick to the
bottom, add a couple of spoonfuls whey or water to prevent that.

While the pumpkin is cooking, dry roast the jeera, fennel, and
coriander seeds on a skillet over a moderate to moderately low heat
for 5 to 6 minutes, tossing and turning the spices with a spatula until they turn a few shades darker and aromatic. Remove the skillet
from the heat, let the spices cool, and grind them into powder.

Add the spinach to the pumpkin. Increase the heat to moderate
and cook, uncovered, for 5 minutes.

Before serving, fold in the roasted spices, nutmeg, kala namak,
and lemon juice. For a richer dish, add cream or homemade sour
cream.

10 oz (250 g) spinach
1–2 Tbsp ghee (page 25) or oil
2 tsp finely grated ginger
  (juice removed)
1 tej patta
1 tsp panch phoron (page 57)
1–2 green chilies, slit
¼ tsp turmeric powder
¼ tsp hing powder
5 cups (1.25 liters) peeled and
  diced pumpkin
¼ cup (63 ml) whey or water,
  or as needed
1½ tsp sea salt, or to taste

TO SERVE
½ tsp jeera
½ tsp fennel
½ tsp coriander seeds
¼ tsp nutmeg powder
½ tsp kala namak
1 Tbsp lemon juice
6 Tbsp cream or homemade
  sour cream (optional,
  page 26)

Carrot and Pumpkin Soup

This soup is as smooth and sweet as cookie dough!
It is a warming appetizer or meal itself with an original flavor and velvety feel.

{SERVES 4}

1–2 Tbsp ghee (page 25),
  butter, or oil
¼ tsp freshly ground black
  pepper
¼ tsp hing powder
1 cup (250 ml) peeled and
  sliced carrots
4 cups (1 liter) peeled and
  diced pumpkin
4 cups (1 liter) water
1 tsp dry roasted panch phoron (page 57) powder
1½ tsp garam masala powder
  (page 58)
¾ tsp sugar
1½–2 tsp sea salt, or to taste
3 Tbsp homemade crème
  fraîche (page 33) or cream

TO SERVE
Handful (20 g) of chopped
  parsley

Heat the ghee, butter, or oil in a pot over moderate heat. When it is hot but not smoking, add the black pepper and hing powder, immediately followed by the carrots. Stir the carrots to coat them evenly with the spices. Fry for 3 to 4 minutes, occasionally mixing, and add the pumpkin cubes. Keep frying for another 3 to 4 minutes.

Add the water and panch phoron powder. Once the mixture is boiling, reduce the heat to moderately low and cook it for 15 to 20 minutes until the vegetables are soft. Remove the pan from the heat and blend the mixture with a immersion blender or food processor until the soup is smooth.

Bring the soup back to the stove, reduce the heat to minimum, add the garam masala, sugar, salt, and crème fraîche or cream; and simmer for 5 minutes.

Garnish with parsley before serving.

Bengali-Style Vegetables
with Ground Mustard Seed

*Looks are deceiving with this dish. Instead of plain and ordinary, it's a carnival of flavors.
Every time I make it, the fragrance transports me to the Bengali countryside of
rice paddies, freely roaming cows, and the distant honking of vehicles.*

*As an alternative cooking technique to the one presented below, you can also roast the potatoes, radish,
beans, and eggplant with a pinch of salt in the oven. Add the blanched spinach to hot ghee or oil after
briefly frying the spices and cook it, uncovered, for a couple of minutes until all liquid has evaporated.
Then fold in the roasted vegetables and season them with the rest of the salt.
Remove the pan from the heat and before serving add the mustard paste to the vegetables.*

*The mustard paste is best ground by hand with chili and water in a stone mortar.
It tends to become bitter if milled electrically.*

{SERVES 4}

10 oz (250 g) spinach
2 cups (500 ml) green beans
12" (5 cm) piece of white
   radish
2–3 medium-size potatoes
1 small eggplant
2–3 Tbsp ghee (page 25) or oil
¾ tsp panch phoron (page 57)
1 tej patta
¼ tsp freshly ground black
   pepper
¼ tsp hing powder
½ tsp turmeric
1¼ tsp sea salt, or to taste
¾ Tbsp black mustard seeds
1–2 green chilies, seeded
1½ tsp organic whole
   cane sugar
2 Tbsp hot water

Wash the spinach in several changes of water to remove dust and
sand. Blanch it in a pot of boiling water for 30 seconds. Drain and
rinse it with cold water to stop the cooking, and chop it coarsely.
Set the spinach aside.

Wash and cut the beans, radish, potatoes, and eggplant into
2-inch (5 cm) long sticks. All the vegetables should be about the
same size. Set them aside.

Heat the ghee in a medium pan or wok over moderate heat.
When it's hot but not smoking, add the panch phoron and tej patta.
As soon as the mustard seeds turn gray and pop, add the black pepper, hing, and turmeric, and then the beans, radish, potatoes, and
eggplant. Fry them, carefully stirring, for 3 to 4 minutes. Then, add
the spinach and salt. Mix well, place the lid slightly ajar, reduce the
heat to moderately low, and simmer until the potatoes are tender
but firm and the liquid has evaporated. Don't stir the vegetables
while cooking. There is no need to add water because the vegetables cook in their own juices. Once turmeric and salt are added, the
vegetables will start to sweat. Spinach is naturally salty and wet.

Meanwhile, grind the mustard seeds, green chili, sugar, and
water into a fine paste.

When the vegetables are tender, increase the heat to moderately high and fry, without stirring, for 4 to 5 minutes until a thin crust forms on the bottom of the pan. Turn off the heat, cover and let the vegetables sit for 5 minutes. It will soften the crust.

Fold in the mustard paste carefully so you do not break the vegetables apart. Serve immediately as a part of a meal with plain rice, dal, and other items.

BREADS, SNACKS & SAVORIES

Poori / 130

Roti / 133

Semolina Crepes / 136

Rice and Dal Crepes / 139

Vada (Lentil Doughnuts) / 142

Avocado Paratha (Bread) / 145

Khandvi / 146

Aloo Bonda / 149

Singara / 150

Yogurt Cheese Pakora / 155

Kale and Cabbage Chips / 156

Poori

Light and flaky, poories are served with chutney as a part of a meal or a snack. Either way, you will find them delightful to eat! Rye flour adds texture and smoky flavor to this dish. If it's not available, substitute spelt or wheat.

{MAKES 10 POORIES}

¾ cup (188 ml) sifted wholegrain spelt flour

¼ cup (63 ml) sifted rye flour

¼ tsp sea salt, or to taste

1 Tbsp melted ghee (page 25), butter, or oil, plus additional for coating

¼–½ cup (63–125 ml) warm water, or as needed

Ghee or oil, for frying

Mix the flours and salt in a bowl. Rub in the ghee, butter, or oil until it resembles a coarse crumble. Add enough warm water to make a firm but pliable dough. Depending on the absorbency of the flour, you may need more or less than ⅓ cup (85 ml). Knead the dough for about 4 or 5 minutes until it is elastic and smooth. Rub the dough with a thin film of ghee, butter, or oil, cover it, and let it rest for at least 20 minutes.

When you are ready to fry the poories, preheat the ghee or oil in a pan or wok over moderate to moderately high heat. There has to be enough ghee or oil to fully cover them during frying. Fill the wok one-third of the way. Deep frying makes the surface bubble and sputter.

The ghee or oil is ready when it is hot but not smoking. To test the temperature, drop a small piece of dough into the wok. It should immediately spring to the top and sizzle.

While the ghee or oil is heating up, roll the dough into 10 equal-size balls between your palms or against a countertop. Place them on a tray or plate brushed with a thin film of ghee or oil. Cover with a damp towel.

Take one ball at a time and roll it into a 4-inch (10–11 cm) disk. Keep the surface oiled to prevent sticking. Carefully slip a disk into the hot ghee or oil. It will sink at first but in a couple of seconds it will spring up. Gently bounce the bread with a slotted spoon in order to make it swell like a balloon. Flip it over and fry the other side for about 30 seconds. Remove the bread and drain it in a colander or sieve or on paper towels. Repeat with the rest of the poories. Serve them immediately, when they are still hot, preferably with a spoonful of chutney.

Roti

*There are many ways to make the flatbreads that are generally called roti.
In this recipe, I use spelt flour, which can be substituted with wheat. Wholegrain flour yields
the healthiest bread, but if you are new to yeast-free baking, start experimenting with a mixture of
wholegrain and all-purpose flour to familiarize yourself with their individual baking qualities.
White flour is more forgiving in many ways; even if you fail to achieve the perfect consistency,
the dough will nonetheless turn into tasty bread.*

*To get rotis to fully puff up takes practice. The dough must be evenly rolled and the timing perfect.
My advice: roll them as thin as possible and keep them on the griddle for a very short time;
otherwise, they will dry up and harden before getting an opportunity to swell with hot air.*

Try thin yogurt, buttermilk, or milk instead of water for a softer texture.

{MAKES ABOUT FIFTEEN 6- TO 7-INCH (15–18 CM) ROTIS}

Mix the flour and salt in a bowl. Add the water gradually while pulling the dough together into an elastic, soft ball with your hand. You may have to adjust the amount of water, depending on the absorbency of the flour. Knead the dough for 5 to 8 minutes, until it is smooth and seamless. The consistency is proper when you poke the dough with a finger and the dough immediately bounces back. If it is too wet, there will be an indentation. Then, knead in a little bit of flour. Cover it with a damp cloth or an upside-down bowl, and set it aside to rest for at least 30 minutes.

When the dough has rested and you are ready to cook, quickly knead it again. Divide it into 14 or 15 parts. Roll each one into a ball between your palms or against a countertop. Place the balls on a floured surface and cover them with a damp cloth.

Take a ball and roll it on the floured surface into a thin, round disk 6 to 7 inches (15–18 cm) across. Add as little flour as possible. Repeat with 3 or 4 more balls and cover them.

2 cups (500 ml) sifted
  wholegrain spelt flour
½ tsp sea salt, or to taste
½–¾ cup (125–188 ml) lukewarm water, or as needed
Melted butter or ghee (page
  25), for brushing the roti

/ Continued /

Making roti requires two sources of heat. Preheat a griddle or cast-iron pan over moderate heat. Turn on another heat source for toasting the bread over a direct flame or heat. Gas stoves work the best, but I've made rotis successfully on electric burners as well. Set an electrical stove on the highest heat and place a wire rack about 1 inch (2.5 cm) above it. The rack should not directly touch the stove; if it does, the bread will burn.

Take one of the disks and shake any excess flour off by tossing it between your palms. Then drop it on the preheated dry pan. As soon as white blisters appear on the surface and the edges curl up, flip it over. You may use a pair of flat tongs instead of your fingers, but be careful not to tear the dough! If the griddle is properly hot, it takes only 30 seconds to cook the first side. Then flip it over. The second side takes even less, just a couple of seconds.

As soon as small air bubbles appear on the second side, lift the roti and place it either in a direct flame (gas) or on a wire rack placed above an electric stove. It should immediately puff with hot air like a balloon. Turn it over. When both sides are cooked and freckled with dark spots, remove the bread from the heat, press out the air and brush it with melted butter or ghee. Repeat with the rest of the dough.

Wrap the bread in a clean cloth, then stack and place it in a preheated oven. Rotis can be kept warm for some time; however, they are best served directly from the pan.

Note: When the rotis are cooked over electric heat, small speckles of flour may sometimes ignite. Don't keep anything flammable, such as a dish towel, next to the stove while cooking.

Semolina Crepes

Making these savory crepes is like applying plaster by hand! There are no hard and fast rules other than liberally spreading the batter on a hot skillet. The crepes are paper thin and full of holes— and they're made that way. They are as delicious as they are amusing to make! Eat them plain or stuff them with delicious fillings and chutneys as a breakfast, snack, or savory side dish to any meal.

{SERVES 4}

¾ cup (188 ml) fine semolina

¾ cup (188 ml) rice flour

¼ cup (63 ml) all-purpose spelt flour

1 tsp sea salt, or to taste

½ tsp freshly ground black pepper

¼ tsp hing powder

1–2 green chilies, seeded and minced

1 tsp finely grated ginger

Handful (20 g) of fresh cilantro, chopped

About 2 cups (500 ml) water, or as needed

Melted ghee (page 25), butter, or oil, for frying

Mix the dry ingredients in a bowl. Add the chilies, ginger, and cilantro. Whisk in the water gradually. The batter should be runny.

Heat a skillet or cast-iron pan over moderate heat. When it is hot, dip your hand in the batter and sprinkle it around the outer edges of the pan. Now, dip your hand again in the batter and sprinkle it toward the center, until the surface of the pan is covered. Repeat, working toward the center, until the surface is covered. If the holes are too large, sprinkle more batter to fill them.

This method of spreading the batter by hand is the best for thin, crisp crepes. If you find it awkward, use a spoon or ladle. Always start filling the surface from the outer edges in a circular motion. The hottest temperature is in the center, so sprinkle the batter there in the end.

After a couple of minutes, add a little bit of melted ghee, melted butter, or oil with a spoon on the sides and top of the crepe. If you have a well-seasoned pan, it won't be necessary other than for flavor. When the crepe is cooked from one side, it will release itself from the pan. The edges will turn upward. Slide a thin spatula underneath and flip it over. If the first side is not cooked properly, the spatula will get stuck underneath. Pull it out carefully and let the crepe fry a little longer. Cook the second side for 1 minute.

Fold the crepes to be eaten as is or fill them and roll them up.

Between frying each crepe, wipe the pan clean with a damp cloth or paper towel.

Rice and Dal Crepes

Nutritious and filling, these paper-thin pancakes are best served piping hot with coconut chutney.
You can also fill them with a simple potato curry or seasoned fresh cheese.

Making them requires planning because fermentation takes time.
Mix a teaspoon of fenugreek seeds with the urad dal. Both of them attract the same kind of
airborne yeast from the environment and thus speed up the fermentation process.

Short grain, hydrated, presteamed, and hulled rice, sold in Indian grocery stores as idli rice, is preferred for
its favorable starch content, but this recipe will work with Arborio rice (an Italian risotto rice) or basmati rice,
too. You can store the fermented batter in the refrigerator for 3 to 4 days and use it in batches.

{MAKES 30 CREPES}

Sort and wash the dal and fenugreek seeds in several changes of water. Place them in a bowl with 3 cups (750 ml) water and soak them for 4 to 5 hours at room temperature.

Sort and wash the rice as well, and soak it in a separate bowl in 4 cups (1 liter) of water for 4 to 5 hours at room temperature.

After 4 or 5 hours, drain the dal and fenugreek seeds. Grind them in a food processor with as little clean water as needed, up to 2 cups (500 ml), to make a smooth paste. Set it aside.

Drain and grind the rice also. Add up to 3 cups (750 ml) clean water. When it's paste-like, add the dal and fenugreek paste to make a thick but airy batter.

I usually grind the dal (with fenugreek) and rice separately and in batches in a small electric spice mill to a very fine texture. Then I combine both in the food processor, which will beat air into the batter. Finally, I may whisk it manually. It is important for fermentation that the batter is light. When the mixture is smooth, transfer it to a large ceramic or glass bowl and whisk it a few times to make sure the batter is thoroughly aerated. Cover it loosely with a lid or plastic wrap and set it aside to ferment.

1 cup (250 ml) split urad dal
1 tsp fenugreek seeds
2 cups (500 ml) idli, Arborio, or basmati rice
12 cups (3 liters) water, divided, plus extra for diluting the batter before frying
2 tsp sea salt, or to taste
Melted ghee (page 25), butter, or oil, for frying

/ Continued /

The ideal temperature for fermentation is above 86°F (30°C) but below 90°F (32°C) where it takes 8 to 12 hours for the batter to ferment. In a lower temperature fermentation may take longer, up to 24 hours. The batter should expand, even double, in volume, become covered with small bubbles, and have a pleasantly sour fragrance. Keep the batter in a draft-free place.

When you are ready to fry the crepes, add the salt and enough water to the mixture so it is the consistency of thick cake batter.

Heat a nonstick frying pan or, preferably, a cast-iron pan over moderate heat. The temperature is correct if drops of water sprinkled on the pan sputter before vanishing. You may use several pans simultaneously to speed up the cooking process.

Place a small ladleful of batter in the center of the pan and quickly spread it in a spiral motion with the back of the ladle to cover the surface. A flat bottom ladle is best for the job. Make the crepe as thin as possible with small ridges. After 30 seconds to a minute, drizzle the edges and top with a spoonful of melted ghee, butter, or oil. Fry 1 to 2 minutes longer until the bottom side is light golden and releases easily from the pan. Flip the crepe over and cook the other side for 30 seconds to 1 minute.

You may have to adjust the temperature between moderate and moderately low if it seems too hot or not hot enough. If the temperature is too high, it's difficult to spread the batter because it hardens too fast and breaks. I usually lift the pan from the heat when I add the batter to make it slightly cooler.

You may keep the crepes in a warm oven and stacked on a plate with the brown side up and lightly covered. If possible, serve directly from the pan.

Vada

(Lentil Doughnuts)

If you find it too cumbersome to form doughnuts by hand, try spooning small balls into the hot ghee or oil with an ice cream scoop. Regardless of the shape, vadas are filling and exciting savory treats. You will find them irresistible when served with both coconut and tamarind chutneys. I like to plunge them in dal or a quick buttermilk broth while eating.

{MAKES ABOUT 20 VADAS}

1 cup (250 ml) split urad dal
¼ tsp turmeric powder
¼ tsp hing powder
4 green chilies
¾–1 tsp sea salt, or to taste
¼ cup (63 ml) water, or as needed
Ghee (page 25) or oil for frying
2 handfuls (40 g) of fresh cilantro, chopped
1 cup (250 ml) finely grated carrot

Sort, wash, and soak the dal for 2 hours. Drain it.

Combine the dal, turmeric, hing, chilies, and salt in a food processor. Run the processor while gradually adding the water through the feed tube. Use only as much water as it takes to make a smooth batter. You may need less than the recipe suggests.

The food processor yields a better result than a blender, which makes the dough too dense. The dough should be airy and light, otherwise the doughnuts will be hard. Just before frying, fold in the chopped cilantro and finely grated carrot.

When you are ready to fry, preheat the ghee or oil in a pan or wok over moderate to moderately high heat. There has to be enough ghee or oil to fully cover the doughnuts during frying. Fill the pan or wok only one-third full. Deep frying makes the surface bubble and sputter. The ghee or oil is ready when hot but not smoking. To test the temperature, drop a small piece of dough into the wok. It should immediately spring to the top and sizzle.

Place a ball of dough the size of a Ping-Pong ball on your left palm (if you are right-handed) and flatten it gently with your right fingers. Keep your hands wet (or smear them with oil) to prevent sticking. Poke a hole in the middle of the flattened dough. Flip the doughnut onto the fingertips of your right hand, then carefully slip it into the hot ghee or oil. It will sink at first but will then spring to the top. Repeat and fry 5 or 6 vadas per batch, depending on the size of your pan or wok. Avoid overcrowding the wok. Turn and gently press the vadas under the surface with a slotted spoon until they puff and become golden on both sides. Remove and drain them in a sieve or colander or on paper towels. Repeat with the remaining dough.

Avocado Paratha
(Avocado Flatbread)

Out of the wide variety of parathas, those made with avocado have the softest and most buttery texture. Make them for breakfast, lunch, or dinner, or as a snack between the meals with chutney while sipping a cup of herbal tea. I like to tear off a piece of paratha, delve into rice and dal— or a vegetable dish—with it, and pop it into my mouth!

{MAKES 6–8 FLATBREADS}

Mix the flours, salt, hing, black pepper, cayenne, and ghee in a bowl.

Puree the avocados with an immersion blender or fork and incorporate them into the flour by hand. The dough should be quite sticky. Add as much lemon juice as needed to attain a proper consistency. Knead the dough for 4 to 5 minutes. Cover and allow it to rest for at least 20 minutes.

Divide the dough into 6 to 8 parts. Roll each part into a ball between your palms or against the counter. Cover the balls again.

When you are ready to fry the dough, preheat a griddle or cast-iron pan over moderate heat. When making a larger quantity, use multiple pans to speed up the process.

Dip a ball of dough into flour and flatten it into a patty between your palms. Carefully roll it out into a 6 to 8-inch (15–20 cm) disk. You may need to sprinkle extra flour while rolling; shake it off before frying.

Place a flatbread on a dry pan. When small air bubbles appear on the top, flip it over. Fry it for about 30 seconds, then brush the top with ghee. As a result, the bread should puff up. Fry it for another minute and flip it over again. Brush it again with ghee. Paratha is ready when both sides have golden reddish crispy spots from contact with the pan. Sprinkle it with chaat masala and remove it from heat. Repeat the process until all the dough is used. Serve parathas piping hot, immediately from the pan.

1 cup (250 ml) sifted wholegrain spelt flour

⅓ cup + 2 Tbsp (115 ml) all-purpose spelt flour plus extra for rolling

1 tsp sea salt, or to taste

¼ tsp hing powder

¼ tsp freshly ground black pepper

¼ tsp cayenne powder

1 Tbsp ghee (page 25), butter, or oil

2 (130 g) peeled, pitted avocados

1½ Tbsp lemon juice, or as needed

Extra flour, for rolling

Melted ghee or butter, for brushing

Chaat masala, for sprinkling on top (page 61)

Khandvi

*Demonstrating the genius of combining simple ingredients, this unusual snack is a
Gujarati delicacy. It's a bit tricky at first to prepare, and may take some trial and error
to get the consistency and cooking procedure right, but when you succeed,
you will be rewarded with a savory snack that melts in your mouth.*

{SERVES 4}

1–2 green chilies, seeded
¾ tsp finely grated ginger
½ cup (125 ml) chickpea flour
½ cup (125 ml) plain yogurt
¼ tsp turmeric powder
Pinch of hing powder
1 tsp sea salt, or to taste
1 cup (250 ml) water

FOR THE TEMPERING
1 Tbsp oil
½ tsp black mustard seeds
1 tsp sesame seeds
20 small fresh curry leaves

TO SERVE
½ cup (125 ml) freshly grated
  coconut
Handful (20 g) of chopped
  cilantro
Pinch of cayenne powder

Start by preparing a large clean metal, glass, or stone surface for
spreading the chickpea flour paste after cooking it. If you have a
wooden or melamine kitchen counter, tear a sheet of foil and place
it on a damp tabletop. A little bit moisture will prevent it from moving when you smear the batter on it.

Grind the chilies and ginger in a spice mill or mortar. Combine
them in a bowl with the chickpea flour, yogurt, the rest of the
spices, and the salt. Add the water gradually and whisk the ingredients until the batter is smooth and silky.

Transfer the mixture into a large, heavy-bottomed pot and bring
it to a boil over a moderately low heat, constantly stirring. As soon
as it starts to thicken, reduce the heat to low. Do not stop stirring
for even a moment! You might want to keep an immersion blender
on hand and run it a couple of times while the mixture is simmering. It will make the batter smooth and glossy.

After simmering the mixture for 10 to 12 minutes, start testing
the consistency by thinly spreading a small amount of the batter on
a metal surface. If it peels off easily after 1 minute, it's ready. If not,
keep simmering, stirring, and repeating the test every few minutes.
You may also test it by placing a drop of batter in a glass of ice-cold
water. It should solidify immediately. If it dissolves, keep simmering.

When the mixture is cooked, turn off the heat immediately,
run the immersion blender for the last time or whisk the batter
vigorously. Then, pour the batter on the prepared surface. Without
delay, spread it with a wide spatula or pastry scraper as thinly and
evenly as possible. Be prepared to work fast because the mixture
settles quickly. Let it cool for 7 to 10 minutes.

Trim the edges and cut 2-inch (5 cm) strips with a knife or pizza
cutter. Pull up the front edge of each strip with a knife and roll it
into a log. Place the rolls on a serving plate and make the tempering.

Heat the oil in a small pan or pot over a moderately high temperature. When it's hot but not smoking, add the mustard seeds. As soon as they turn gray and pop, add the sesame seeds. When they turn a shade darker, add the curry leaves. When they become brittle, turn off the heat and pour the tempering evenly over the khandvi rolls.

Garnish with the fresh coconut, cilantro, and a sprinkle of cayenne powder. Serve within a couple of hours as a snack or side dish. Khandvi becomes moist and soggy when stored even until the next day. If you don't serve it immediately, keep it refrigerated and add the tempering and garnish right before plating.

Aloo Bonda

Aloo bondas are battered, fried potato balls. They are typically served as finger food or snacks. Try them with coconut, tamarind, or tomato chutney. You can fill dosas (rice and lentil crepes) with this same basic potato recipe. If serving it as a filling, leave the potatoes coarser after mashing them.

{MAKES 20 BALLS}

Mix the chickpea and rice flours, spices, ½ teaspoon salt, and water in a bowl. It should be the consistency of cake batter. If it's too runny, add more chickpea flour. Otherwise it won't coat the potato balls properly. Set the batter aside.

Wash and boil the potatoes with skins on until they are soft. When still hot, peel and mash them coarsely with a fork.

Heat the ghee or oil on a skillet or pan over moderate heat. When it's hot but not smoking, add the ginger (juice removed). When it turns light golden, add the mustard seeds. As soon as they turn gray and pop, add the chilies, turmeric, and hing powder immediately followed by the mashed potatoes and peas. Add the remaining 1 teaspoon salt, decrease the heat to low, and cook, covered, until the peas are soft. Lightly mash the peas with a back of a spoon or spatula. Set the mixture aside and let it cool.

Roll the potato mixture into 20 balls. Set them aside.

Heat the ghee or oil in a pan or wok over moderate heat. You'll need enough ghee or oil to fully cover the balls during frying. Fill the pan or wok only one-third full. Deep frying will make the surface bubble and sputter.

The ghee or oil is ready when it is hot but not smoking. To test the temperature, drop a small piece of batter into the wok. It should immediately spring to the top and sizzle.

Use a spoon or an ice cream scoop to dip the balls into the batter. Remove one first and dip it into the hot ghee or oil. Fry the balls in batches. Use a slotted spoon to rotate and move them. It takes only 2 to 3 minutes to fry them. Drain them in a sieve or colander or on paper towels. Like most fried foods, aloo bonda is best served immediately. You may keep it warm and crisp in a preheated oven at 275°F (136 C°) for up to 30 minutes.

1 cup (250 ml) chickpea flour
1 Tbsp rice flour
¾ tsp cayenne powder
½ tsp turmeric powder
1½ tsp sea salt, or to taste
½–¾ cup (125–188 ml) water
1 lb (500 g) potatoes
1–2 Tbsp ghee (page 25) or oil
1 Tbsp finely grated ginger (juice removed)
½ tsp black mustard seeds
2–3 green chilies, seeded and minced
¼ tsp turmeric powder
¼ tsp hing powder
¾ cup (188 ml) green peas
Ghee or oil, for deep frying

Singara

Every culture has a version of a savory handpie, similar to a samosa.
It's enjoyed as a snack or lunch box food. In Bengal, it's called a singara.
You can see them made fresh by street vendors all around the region.

My interpretation has tiny bits of potatoes, cauliflower florets, and peas
enveloped in a flaky crust made of spelt flour. Traditionally, refined wheat is used for the dough.
This recipe is for deep-fried singaras, but you may bake them in the oven instead.
In that case, brush them with milk, yogurt, or water, and bake them on the middle rack
of the oven at 425°F (220°C) until they are a golden color, about 15 to 20 minutes.

{MAKES 28 APPETIZER-SIZE SINGARAS}

FOR THE DOUGH
1 cup (250 ml) whole grain spelt
    flour
1 cup (250 ml) all-purpose spelt
    flour
¾ tsp sea salt, or to taste
3 Tbsp ghee (page 25)
6–8 Tbsp lukewarm water,
    or as needed

FOR THE FILLING
2 cups (500 ml) very small cauli-
    flower florets
1 cup (250 ml) tiny potato cubes
¼ cup (63 ml) water, for
    steaming
2 tsp panch phoron (page 57)
2–3 Tbsp ghee or oil
2 tsp fresh, finely grated
    ginger (juice removed)
1 tej patta
2–3 green chilies, seeded and
    minced

⅓ tsp freshly ground black
    pepper
⅓ tsp hing powder
¾ cup (188 ml) green peas,
    fresh or frozen
⅓ tsp turmeric powder
¾ tsp garam masala powder
    (page 58)
1 tsp kala namak powder
1 tsp sugar
1 tsp sea salt, or to taste
1½ Tbsp lemon juice
3 Tbsp desiccated coconut
3 Tbsp coarsely powdered,
    roasted peanuts
Handful (20 g) of fresh cilantro,
    chopped
Ghee or oil for, frying

TO SERVE
Chaat masala, to garnish
    (page 61)

/ Continued /

Mix the flours and salt in a bowl. Rub in the ghee with your fingers until the mixture resembles coarse crumbs. Add the water gradually while pulling the dough together into a ball with your hand. The exact amount of water depends on the absorbency of flour. You may use more or less than the recipe calls for. The ideal consistency is pliable but firm. Knead the dough until it forms a smooth, elastic ball. Cover and let it rest for at least 30 minutes.

Steam the cauliflower and potato pieces in a pot with the water over moderately low heat for 5 to 7 minutes until they are almost cooked but still firm. The water should completely absorb and evaporate. Drain and set aside.

Dry roast the panch phoron seeds in a skillet or pan over moderately low heat, tossing and turning them with a spatula for 5 to 6 minutes. Remove the seeds from the heat and let them cool. Grind them into powder and set it aside.

Heat the ghee or oil in a wok or pan over moderate heat. When it's hot but not smoking, add the grated ginger (juice removed) and tej patta. Fry, tossing and turning the spices with a spatula until the ginger turns light golden. Add the chilies, black pepper, and hing immediately followed by the steamed potato bits and cauliflower florets. Mix to coat the vegetables evenly with the spices. Reduce the heat to moderately low. Fry the vegetables for 5 to 6 minutes until they are cooked and golden on all sides. Add the peas and mix. Turn off the heat after 2 minutes. Remove the tej patta.

Combine the vegetables with the turmeric, garam masala, kala namak, sugar, salt, lemon juice, coconut, peanuts, and fresh cilantro. Let the mixture cool before making the singaras.

Knead the dough briefly and roll it into a log. Divide the log into 14 equal-size portions. Roll each one into a smooth ball. Cover.

When you are ready to fry, preheat the ghee or oil in a wok or pan over moderate heat. There should be at least 2 inches (5 cm) of ghee or oil on the bottom of the pan, and one-third of the pot should be empty. When you slip the singaras into the wok, the ghee or oil will bubble and sputter. The empty space prevents an overflow.

The ghee or oil is ready when hot but not smoking. To test the temperature, drop a small piece of dough into the wok. It should immediately spring to the top and sizzle.

While the ghee or oil is heating up, take a ball of dough and roll it into a 5-by-6-inch (12 × 15 cm) oblong disk. Cut it in half width-wise. Take one half and fold it into a cone by overlapping the cut edges and pinching them tightly together. Rest the cone between your thumb and forefinger while stuffing it. Press the filling lightly down and leave some space around the outer edges. Now, pinch the edges tightly together. You may crimp them or make a decorative border. In either case, the objective is to have the singara securely closed; otherwise, it will open when fried. Repeat this process with the rest of the dough.

Slide the singaras carefully, one by one, into the hot ghee or oil. The safest way is to use a metal spoon instead of your hands. Avoid overcrowding the pan. Fry them in batches.

It takes about 3 to 5 minutes to thoroughly fry the singaras. Gently move and turn them with a slotted spoon for an even result. They should be light, float on the top, and be golden in color. Try to keep the temperature steady and moderate.

When they are ready, lift them with a slotted spoon and drain them in a sieve or colander or on paper towels.

Sprinkle the singaras with chaat masala and serve them hot or at room temperature.

Yogurt Cheese Pakora

This recipe features a basic, versatile fritter batter made of chickpea and rice flour.
Use it to coat any vegetables, leaves, herbs, or flowers before frying. You may add spices,
like ground jeera, coriander, or garam masala, to it.

For frying yogurt cheese, the batter must be fairly thick in order to prevent the cheese
from escaping from the fritter during deep frying. For vegetables, leave the batter thinner.
Adjust the amount of salt and spices according to your taste.

{SERVES 4}

Mix the flours, spices, and salt. Add the water gradually while vigorously whisking the batter. It should have the consistency of thick cream. Adjust the amount of water accordingly. Set the batter aside to rest for at least 20 minutes.

Combine the yogurt cheese, spices, salt, and herbs in a separate bowl. Use a spoon or an ice cream scoop to roll small balls. Place them on a plate in the freezer or refrigerator until you are ready to fry them. The colder they are, the better they retain their shape when dipped into the batter.

Heat the ghee or oil in a pot or wok over moderate heat. There should be at least 2 inches (5 cm) ghee or oil in the pan in order to fully cover the pakoras. Leave one-third of the pan empty. The hot ghee or oil will bubble and sputter, when you slip the pakoras into the pan. The empty space prevents an overflow.

The ghee or oil is ready when it is hot but not smoking. To test the temperature, drop a small piece of dough into the wok. It should immediately spring to the top and sizzle.

Drop a ball into the batter. Coat it evenly, then carefully slide it with the help of a spoon into the hot ghee or oil. Repeat, frying the pakoras in batches without overcrowding the wok. Use a slotted spoon to move and turn the balls. When they are light golden on all sides, in about 30 seconds, remove and drain them in a colander or sieve or on paper towels.

Serve with chutney as a side dish or as a snack.

FOR THE BATTER
1 cup (250 ml) chickpea flour
  (besan)
½ cup (125 ml) rice flour
½ tsp cayenne powder
¼ tsp turmeric powder
1½ tsp sea salt, or to taste
½–¾ cup (125–188 ml) cold
  water

FOR THE YOGURT CHEESE
1½ cups (375 ml) yogurt
  cheese (page 37)
¾ tsp freshly ground black
  pepper
2 fresh, long red chilies,
  seeded and minced
¾ tsp kala namak powder
⅓ tsp sea salt, or to taste
Handful (20 g) of basil leaves,
  minced
Ghee (page 25) or oil,
  for frying

Kale and Cabbage Chips

*Kale is high in beta-carotene, vitamins K and C, and calcium. Dehydration leads to only a
nominal nutritional loss, and the consistency becomes similar to potato chips.
Like other brassicas, it contains sulforaphane, a chemical compound with potent anticancer properties.
For variety, combine kale with savoy cabbage. You may also try beet greens
and kohlrabi, broccoli, or Brussels sprout plant leaves.*

{MAKES 20 LARGE CHIPS, WHICH YOU CAN BREAK INTO SMALLER BITES}

10 curly kale leaves
10 savoy cabbage leaves
Pinch of hing powder
Pinch of freshly ground
 black pepper
Pinch of Himalaya salt
2 Tbsp olive, coconut, or
 avocado oil

Preheat the oven to 250°F (125°C).

Wash the kale and cabbage leaves and pat them dry with a clean
towel. Remove the tough parts of the stems. You can either chop
the leaves into bite-size pieces or leave them large. Sprinkle the
leaves with the spices, salt, and oil. Transfer them to a baking sheet
in a single layer and bake them for 30 minutes until they are crisp.
When they are cool to touch, transfer them to a serving bowl.

SALADS, SEEDLINGS
& SPROUTS

Fenugreek Leaves / 160

Chickpea Rice Salad with Cashews and Microgreens / 163

Herb Salad with Pea Shoots and Pistachio / 164

Summer Salad with Edible Flowers / 167

Watermelon Salad with Toasted Sunflower Seeds / 168

Wilted Green Salad / 171

Red Cabbage, Beets, and Avocado Salad / 172

Braised Artichoke Salad / 175

Steamed Vegetable Salad / 176

Fenugreek Leaves

It is very easy to grow your own seedlings and leaves on a windowsill. One of my favorite to grow is fenugreek, which germinates within 12 hours and is ready to be harvested within a week or two.

Place organic soil in a traylike container or pot, and water it thoroughly. Sprinkle a generous amount of seeds on the top. There is no need to cover them with soil.

Place the container on a windowsill, and spray the seedlings daily with fresh water. They will grow roots almost instantly and develop a set of small leaves. You can trim and use these first leaves (and stalks) in salads or wait until they mature and develop clover-shaped darker foliage with three leaves on the top. Fully grown, the fenugreek reaches 12 to 24 inches (30–60 cm) in height.

You can harvest and eat both the young seedlings and the clover-shaped leaves with soft stalks intact. Once the stalks harden, discard them.

Add fresh fenugreek leaves to any flatbread dough, dal, or rice. Slightly bitter and nutty, the leaves shine with potatoes and grant an aroma like that of fennel or celery. Use them as vegetables along with spinach and other leafy greens.

Involve your kids in planting a window garden! They will love to see tiny sprouts growing into food. Try kale, cabbage, broccoli, cauliflower, Brussels sprouts, and kohlrabi seeds, too. They germinate almost as quickly as fenugreek.

Chickpea Rice Salad with Cashews and Microgreens

Because fenugreek seeds germinate so readily in a wet soil on a windowsill, it's possible to harvest a new batch of sprouts once a week throughout the year. Use them as such in salads or add a handful to dal, vegetables, or bread dough. Here, I've paired them with other microgreens, chickpeas, cashew nuts, and rice. See how to grow fenugreek leaves on page 160.

{SERVES 4}

Wash and sort the chickpeas, removing any stones. Soak the chickpeas in plenty of filtered water overnight. Drain.

Bring the water to a boil in a medium pan or pot over high heat. When it's boiling, add the soaked chickpeas, tej patta, and cinnamon stick. Reduce the heat to moderate. As soon as white foam appears on the top, skim it off and add a tablespoon of ghee or oil. Cook the chickpeas, covered, for an hour or until soft but not mushy. Drain and set them aside.

Whisk together the olive oil, lemon juice, black pepper, hing, paprika, kala namak, and salt in a small bowl, or shake the ingredients in a covered jar. Add the mixture to the cooked chickpeas. (You may do this step in advance: marinate the chickpeas in the refrigerator overnight.) Mix the chickpeas with the cooked rice, roasted cashews, microgreens, and fenugreek seedlings just before serving.

½ cup (125 ml) chickpeas
8 cups (2 liters) water
1 tej patta
3" (7.5 cm) piece of cinnamon stick or cassia bark
1 Tbsp ghee (page 25) or oil

FOR THE DRESSING
2–3 Tbsp extra virgin olive oil
2 Tbsp lemon juice
1 tsp freshly ground black pepper
¼ tsp hing powder
1 tsp sweet paprika powder
2 tsp kala namak powder
2 tsp sea salt, or to taste

3 cups (750 ml) cooked basmati rice
¼ lb (100 g) roasted cashew nuts
3 handfuls (60 g) of microgreens such as amaranth, mustard, baby spinach, etc. (see page 273)
Handful (20 g) of fenugreek leaves (see page 160)

Herb Salad with
Pea Shoots and Pistachio

This fresh summer salad can be made on a whim, capturing the lightness of the season.
To make it more substantial, add cooked beans (azuki beans, black-eyed peas, black beans,
lima beans, navy beans, pinto beans, chickpeas, or lentils) or paneer to the greens.

{SERVES 4}

1 head of lettuce
Generous handful of pea
   shoots
Generous handful of basil
   leaves
Handful of dill
Handful of parsley leaves
Handful of roasted pistachio
   nuts
¼ cup (63 ml) extra virgin
   olive oil
3 Tbsp lemon juice
¼ tsp freshly ground black
   pepper
Pinch of hing powder
Pinch of sea salt, or to taste

Wash and drain the lettuce, sprouts, and herbs. Pat them dry with a towel if water clings to the leaves. Combine them with a handful of pistachios in a bowl. Sprinkle them with extra virgin olive oil, lemon juice, black pepper, hing powder, and salt. Serve immediately.

Summer Salad with Edible Flowers

The taste of edible flowers such as calendula, carnation, chamomile, cress, dill, jasmine, lavender, lilacs, marjoram, and squash blossoms varies from sweet to peppery to pungent. Such flowers add a splash of color to the table. Use them cautiously if you have pollen or other flower allergies and always refer to a botanical guidebook before introducing flowers into your diet. Many flowers are unsuitable for consumption.

{SERVES 4}

Wash, peel, and cut the cucumbers into 2-inch-long (5 cm) and 1-inch-wide (2.5 cm) sticks. Wash, peel, and cut the kohlrabi into 2-inch-long (5 cm) and ½-inch-wide (7 mm) sticks. Wash and peel the radishes. Wash the edible flowers. Set everything aside to dry.

Dry roast the pine nuts in a skillet or pan over moderate to moderately low heat until they become golden on all sides. Set them aside to cool.

Wash, peel, and pit the avocado. Combine it with the lemon zest, yogurt, olive oil, spices, salt, and mint in a blender or food processor. Process the dressing until it becomes smooth.

Arrange the salad on a plate or platter by spooning the dressing on the bottom and layering the cucumbers, kohlrabi, flowers, and pine nuts on top.

1 cucumber
1 kohlrabi
10–12 radishes
Handful of edible flowers
3 Tbsp pine nuts

FOR THE DRESSING
1 avocado
Zest of an organic lemon
½ cup (125 ml) natural yogurt
¼ cup (63 ml) extra virgin olive oil
½ tsp freshly ground black pepper
¼ tsp cayenne pepper
1 tsp kala namak powder
½ tsp sea salt, or to taste
Handful (20 g) of fresh mint leaves

Watermelon Salad with Toasted Sunflower Seeds

Watermelon is best eaten on an empty stomach or at the beginning of a meal.
It digests faster than most foods and may cause irregularities if mixed with cooked items.

{SERVES 4}

1 watermelon just over 1 lb
  (500 g)
¾ cups (188 ml) yogurt
  cheese (see page 37)
Handful (20 g) of fresh basil
  leaves
Handful (20 g) of fresh mint
  leaves
2–3 Tbsp extra virgin olive
  oil
Pinch of kala namak
Pinch of sea salt, or to taste

FOR THE TOASTED
  SUNFLOWER SEEDS
1 tsp oil
¼ lb (100 g) sunflower seeds
Pinch of hing powder
Pinch of freshly ground
  black pepper
Pinch of cayenne powder
Pinch of salt

Wash, peel, and slice the watermelon. Arrange the slices on a
platter or plate. Place a little bit of yogurt cheese on the top of each
slice.

Wash the fresh basil and mint leaves. Chop and sprinkle them
over the watermelon with the olive oil, kala namak, and salt.

Heat the oil in a skillet or pan over moderate heat. Add the sunflower seeds, spices, and salt. Roast, constantly tossing and turning
the spices with a spatula until the seeds are golden. Top the salad
with them before serving.

Wilted Green Salad

From early spring to late summer, various greens and edible weeds are available,
from dandelion to garden chards, changing week by week. Whether you blanch, steam, or boil them,
they guarantee an energy boost. For this recipe, I suggest you sauté Swiss chard and turnip tops
in ghee or butter and serve them with lemon wedges. You may also use the young leaves of beets, kohlrabi,
broccoli, Brussels sprouts, and radishes. Remember to cook bitter greens, like chicory, longer than sweet ones.
Consult a botanical guidebook before gathering wild edibles.

{SERVES 4}

Trim and discard the unusable parts of each vegetable. Wash the stalks and leaves in several changes of water to remove any dust and dirt. Drain and chop the vegetables.

Heat the ghee or butter in a pan over moderate heat. Add the stalks and cook them, tossing and turning them for 7 to 8 minutes until they are fork-tender. Then add the leaves and continue cooking for 1 or 2 minutes until they wilt. Remove the pan from the heat.

Sprinkle the greens with black pepper and salt, and serve them immediately with lemon wedges.

1 pound (500 g) greens (spinach, chard, arugula, beet, and turnip tops or edible wild leaves and weeds)
1–2 Tbsp ghee (page 25) or butter

TO SERVE
Generous pinch of freshly ground black pepper
Generous pinch of salt
Lemon wedges

Red Cabbage, Beets, and Avocado Salad

Like most of the salads in this chapter, this one represents the essence of fresh food.
It's vibrant, revitalizing, and most important, can be thrown together with ingredients you likely
have on hand. The little bit of this and that can vary according to what is available.
One day it may be a red cabbage; another day a bunch of kohlrabi, carrots, or zucchini.

{SERVES 4}

Quarter of a small
  red cabbage
2 medium-size boiled beets
2 avocados
Half of 1 fresh coconut
½ tsp ghee (page 25) or oil
Pinch each of hing, black
  pepper, cayenne, and salt
½ cup (125 ml) sunflower
  seeds

FOR THE DRESSING
2 Tbsp lemon juice
2 Tbsp orange juice
¼ cup (63 ml) extra virgin
  olive oil
Handful (20 g) of fresh
  parsley
Handful (20 g) of fresh dill
Pinch each of hing, black
  pepper, and sugar
¾ tsp kala namak powder
¼ tsp sea salt, or to taste

Wash the vegetables. Shave the cabbage into thin ribbons with a sharp knife. Peel and dice the beets. Peel, pit, and dice the avocados. Shred the coconut. Set everything in a bowl.

Heat the ghee or oil in a skillet or pan over moderately low heat. Add the spices, salt, and sunflower seeds. Roast the seeds for 5 to 7 minutes until they turn light golden. Combine the seeds and the vegetables.

Make the dressing by placing the juices, olive oil, herbs, spices, and salt in a blender. Pulse a few times and pour the dressing over the salad just before serving.

Braised Artichoke Salad

Once the outer leaves of the artichoke are removed, its tender heart is revealed. It is covered by a beard and sharp, pointed leaves that you must scrape out before eating. Clean artichokes before cooking. Although the stem and outer leaves are edible, they are often too fibrous and hard to chew. However, I like to boil as much of the vegetable as possible and discard the tough parts while eating. Leaves, for example, have a fleshy base that would be a shame to waste.

The cut edges turn brown quickly. Chop them fast and plunge them immediately into a mixture of lemon juice and water. This acidulated mixture will stop the oxidization.

Drizzle the cooked artichokes with extra virgin olive oil and serve them as a side dish or on a bed of greens.

{SERVES 4}

Wash the artichokes, lemons, and dill. Cut the lemons in quarters. Fill a bowl with water and squeeze the juice of the lemon quarters. Reserve the peel.

Remove the tough end of the artichoke stems. Usually 1 inch (2.5 cm) is left intact. Snap off the bottom three layers of leaves and rub the cut surfaces with the reserved lemon peel. Use a serrated knife to cut off the top part of the artichoke. Then trim the base and peel the stem. Rub the surfaces with lemon as you go. Split the artichoke in half. Place the part you are not working with into the bowl of lemon water.

Scrape off and discard the beard and pointed leaves in the center. Repeat this process with the rest of the artichokes.

Transfer the artichokes and the lemon water into a pot. You may need to add more water, depending on the size of the pot. The vegetables should be almost covered.

Add the olive oil, salt, and dill, and bring the water to a boil over high heat. As soon as it boils, reduce the heat to low or moderately low and simmer for 20 to 30 minutes until the artichokes are cooked. Remove from the heat, drain, and allow them to cool.

Before serving, sprinkle with extra virgin olive oil.

2 large artichokes
2 lemons
5–6 stalks fresh dill
3 Tbsp extra virgin olive oil plus extra for garnish
1 tsp sea salt, or to taste
Extra virgin olive oil

Steamed Vegetable Salad

Although delicious when still warm, this main course salad boasts flavors that intensify upon cooling. Therefore, you can make it ahead of time, keep it in the refrigerator, and serve it cold within 12 hours— the perfect summer treat. Almost all vegetables are suitable for the salad. Choose them according to a similar cook time or cut smaller the ones that take longer to cook. You can also steam the vegetables successively, starting from the harder ones and dropping in the softer ones later.

{SERVES 4 TO 6}

1½ lbs (700 g) mixed vegetables (such as baby potatoes, broccoli, cauliflower, carrots, and beans)

½ cup (125 ml) water, or as needed for steaming

2 cups (500 ml) natural yogurt

1 cup (250 ml) sour cream

¼ cup (63 ml) extra virgin olive oil

¼ tsp hing powder

1 tsp freshly ground black pepper

1 tsp kala namak powder

1½ tsp sea salt, or to taste

1 handful (20 g) of fresh dill, chopped

2 handfuls (40 g) of fresh basil, chopped

Wash all the vegetables. Cut the cauliflower or broccoli into florets, potatoes into cubes, and carrots and beans into sticks that are the same length.

Pour water into a pot to cover the bottom and bring it to a boil over high heat. As soon as it boils, reduce the heat to moderately low and add the vegetables. You may want to add the beans a bit later because their cooking time is only 3 to 4 minutes. Cover and steam until they are fork-tender but not mushy. Drain and refresh the vegetables by rinsing them immediately with cold water.

Mix the yogurt, sour cream, olive oil, spices, salt, and herbs in a bowl. Combine the yogurt mixture with the vegetables.

Serve warm, cold, or at room temperature.

CHUTNEYS, RAITAS & SAUCES

Cashew Chutney / 180

Coconut Chutney / 181

Date and Tamarind Chutney / 183

Gooseberry Chutney / 184

Plum Chutney / 187

Apple Chutney / 188

Tomato Chutney / 191

Tomato Sauce with Saffron / 192

Quick Eggplant Pickles / 195

Banana Raita / 196

Eggplant Raita / 197

Cashew Chutney

*Prepared with digestive ingredients, like ginger and lemon or lime, raw chutneys such as
this cashew version boost the appetite. If you want to use it as a salad dressing, thin it with water.
By substituting the cashews with raw or roasted peanuts or pine nuts, you get another flavor.
Try yogurt in place of water and lemon juice for a creamier result.*

{MAKES 1½ CUPS (375 ML)}

1 cup (250 ml) cashew nuts
2 green chilies, seeded and
minced
1 Tbsp grated ginger
Pinch smoked paprika
½ tsp sea salt, or to taste
1 tsp lemon juice
About ½ cup (125 ml) water,
  or as needed

TO SERVE
2 Tbsp chopped, fresh cilantro

Place all the ingredients except the cilantro in a blender or food
processor and blend them until the chutney becomes smooth.
Transfer it to a serving bowl and add the cilantro. Serve a spoonful
as a relish for a main meal, or dip any bread, cracker, or chip into it
when snacking.

Store the chutney in a lidded jar in the refrigerator for not longer than 2 or 3 days.

Coconut Chutney

The mild heat in this simple coconut chutney is from cayenne. Uncooked, it's a quick relish to make. It pairs well with any fried bread or savory but is especially soothing with rice and lentil crepes filled with spicy potatoes. The flavors infuse upon storing the chutney in the refrigerator, and you can safely make it a day ahead.

{MAKES 2½ CUPS (625 ML)}

Combine all the ingredients in a food processor and pulse a couple of times, until smooth. Transfer the chutney into a serving bowl. Store in a lidded jar in the refrigerator for not longer than 2 or 3 days.

1 cup (250 ml) fresh or desiccated coconut
1 tsp cayenne powder
1½ tsp organic whole cane sugar
¾–1 tsp sea salt, or to taste
1½ cups (375 ml) homemade yogurt (page 34)
Handful (20g) of fresh mint leaves, chopped

Date and Tamarind Chutney

This sweet and tart condiment with complex flavors goes well with any fried savories, but it shines with lentil doughnuts (page 142), especially when served together with coconut chutney.

{MAKES 3–4 CUPS (750 ML–1 LITER)}

Combine the dates with the tamarind concentrate, sugar or jaggery, ginger slices, and water in a pan or pot. Bring the water to a boil over high heat. Then, reduce the heat to moderately low and cook, uncovered, for 30 minutes until the chutney thickens. Press it through a sieve and discard the ginger slices. If the chutney is too thick to your taste, dilute it with freshly squeezed lemon or orange juice to your taste.

Add the chaat masala, cayenne, and salt. Mix well and let the flavors steep—preferably overnight in the refrigerator—before serving. Store in a lidded jar in the refrigerator for not longer than 2 or 3 days.

40–45 Medjool dates, pitted and peeled
3 Tbsp tamarind concentrate
¾ cup (188 ml) organic whole cane sugar or jaggery
1" (2.5 cm) piece of fresh ginger, peeled and sliced
2 cups (500 ml) water
1 tsp chaat masala (page 61)
¼ tsp cayenne powder
½ tsp salt

Gooseberry Chutney

*This chutney is on the sweet side: something to serve at the end of dinner in place of a dessert.
If you wish to increase heat, briefly fry 1 or 2 chilies with the tej patta and cinnamon stick
in a tablespoon of ghee in a pot before adding the berries, lime juice, and sugar.
Continue cooking as instructed below. Use either red or green European gooseberries.
Both turn deep burgundy when cooked.*

{MAKES 3–4 CUPS (750 ML–I LITER)}

4 cups (1 liter) red or green
    gooseberries
3 Tbsp lime juice
2 cups (500 ml) sugar
1 tsp cayenne powder
1 small tej patta
2" (5 cm) piece of cinnamon
    stick or cassia bark
½ tsp panch phoron (page 57)
¼ tsp sea salt, or to taste
1 tsp chaat masala (page 61)

Destem the berries and wash them. Place them in a pot with the lime juice, sugar, cayenne, tej patta, and cinnamon stick.

Bring the mixture to a boil over high heat. As soon as it starts boiling, reduce the heat to low and simmer, covered, for 40 to 60 minutes. Shake the pan occasionally to prevent scorching.

In the meantime dry roast the panch phoron seeds on a pan over moderately low heat for 4 to 5 minutes until they turn slightly darker and aromatic. Remove them from the heat and let them cool. Grind into powder and set aside.

When the chutney has cooked for about an hour, add the panch phoron powder and simmer it, uncovered, for 5 to 10 minutes. Then, remove the pan from the heat. Some of the berries should have broken and some of them should remain whole.

Discard the whole spices and add the salt and chaat masala.

The chutney continues to thicken as it cools down. In the refrigerator it will become jam-like. Store in a lidded jar in the refrigerator for not longer than 2 or 3 days.

Plum Chutney

*I make this late summer favorite from purple or red plums on the occasion of Radhasthami—
one of the holiest festivals of the year, during which bhakti-yogis glorify the most devoted servant
of Sri Krishna, Srimati Radharani, and pray for her grace. As she is the epitome of all
admirable feminine qualities from sweetness to the ability to control with love, this caramel-scented,
tangy plum chutney is named after her as Radha Red.*

*In the wintertime, you can use prunes for equally delicious chutney. In that case,
soak the prunes beforehand and add water to the recipe to reach the desired consistency.
You may have to reduce the amount of sugar because dried fruits are naturally sweet.*

{MAKES ABOUT 4 CUPS (1 LITER)}

Wash, dry, pit, and slice the plums into quarters. Set them aside.

Heat the ghee or oil in a pan or pot over moderate heat. When it is hot but not smoking, add the grated ginger (juice removed) and green chilies. Toss and fry the ginger until it turns light golden. Add the powdered spices immediately followed by the plums. Stir to coat the fruits with the spices and add the juices and orange zest. Bring the mixture to a boil, then reduce the heat to moderately low and cook, covered, for 8 to 10 minutes until the plums are soft.

Add the sugar. Cook for 12 to 15 minutes longer until the chutney thickens and reaches a thin jam-like consistency. It will further thicken as it cools. Remove the pan from heat, discard the chili pods, and add the salt.

Serve warm or at room temperature as a side to a main meal, or with any fried savory. Plum chutney is especially delicious with poories (page 130). Store in a lidded jar in the refrigerator for not longer than 2 or 3 days.

25 oz (700 g) plums
1–2 Tbsp ghee (page 25) or oil
2 tsp finely grated ginger
  (juice removed)
2 green chilies, split
1 tsp coriander powder
¼ tsp cinnamon powder
¼ tsp clove powder
¼ tsp cardamom powder
¼ tsp nutmeg powder
Juice of 1 orange
Juice of ½ lemon
Zest of 1 orange
2 cups (500 ml) sugar
¼–½ tsp sea salt

Apple Chutney

Tart, starchy apples work best for this recipe, but you can modify it by using almost any other fruit.
Try peaches, nectarines, apricots, pears, or mangoes instead of apples. You can also mix fruits and berries,
or even fresh and dried fruits such as raisins, pineapple, and papaya. Increase the amount of sugar
if you cook with a tarter fruit and decrease it if you add dried fruits that have concentrated sugar content.

{MAKES 2–3 CUPS (500–750 ML)}

6–7 peeled, cored tart apples
1–2 Tbsp ghee (page 25) or oil
¼ tsp anise or jeera seeds
3" (7.5 cm) stick of cinnamon
1 Tbsp finely grated ginger
1–2 green chilies, slit
¼ cup (63 ml) orange juice
½–¾ cup (125–188 ml) sugar,
  or to taste

Wash, peel, core, and cut the apples into small chunks. Set the fruit aside.

Heat the ghee or oil in a pan or pot over moderate heat. When it's hot but not smoking, add the anise or jeera seeds and cinnamon stick. Fry the spices, tossing and turning them with a spatula until the spices are slightly darker, about 30 seconds. Add the ginger and chilies. Fry for 1 minute and add the apple chunks. Coat them evenly with the spices and fry them for 6 to 7 minutes or until they are fairly soft.

Stir in the orange juice and sugar. Adjust the amount of sugar according to the sourness of the fruit. Reduce the heat to low, cover the pot, and cook, occasionally mixing, for 15 minutes. Then increase the heat to moderate again and cook, constantly stirring, for 5 minutes until the chutney becomes jam-like. Turn off the heat and remove the cinnamon stick and chilies.

If you prefer smooth chutney without chunks of fruit, add the orange juice after sautéing the apples in ghee and spices, and cook for about 10 minutes until the apples turn soft and form a thick applesauce. Finally, add the sugar, reduce the heat to low, and simmer the mixture 15 minutes longer.

Serve the chutney warm, cold, or at room temperature. Store in a lidded jar in the refrigerator for not longer than 2 or 3 days.

Tomato Chutney

*When there are plenty of tomatoes available in the late summer, this chutney is a must.
It's sweet and rich and partners with savory treats and full meals alike. For a change,
try it with kitchari (see page 79)! Use organic whole cane sugar for a deep and
dark spirit or refined sugar for a lighter note.*

{MAKES 2–3 CUPS (500–750 ML)}

Wash, peel, and remove the stems from the tomatoes. Quarter them and set them aside.

Wash and drain the raisins. Set them aside.

Heat the ghee or oil in a pan or pot over moderate heat. When it's hot but not smoking, add the grated ginger (juice removed), chilies, and tej patta. Fry the spices, tossing and turning them with a spatula, until the ginger turns light golden. Then, add the panch phoron seeds and fry them for 20 to 30 seconds. Add the tomato quarters, raisins, and turmeric. Reduce the heat to moderately low and cook, covered, for 15 to 20 minutes until the tomatoes are tender.

In the meantime, dry roast the fennel seeds in a skillet or pan over moderate to moderately low heat until they become a few shades darker and aromatic, for 5 to 6 minutes. Remember to toss and turn the pan to evenly toast the spices! Remove the spices from the heat and let them cool. Grind into powder.

Add the sugar, fennel powder, and salt to the chutney. Reduce the heat to minimum and cook for 5 to 7 minutes, uncovered, until the chutney becomes thick and plump.

Let the chutney cool to room temperature and remove the tej patta and chilies before serving. Store in a lidded jar in the refrigerator for not longer than 2 or 3 days.

8–10 medium-size tomatoes
3 Tbsp raisins or sultanas
3 Tbsp ghee (page 25) or oil
1 Tbsp fresh, grated ginger (juice removed)
1–3 green chilies, slit
1 tej patta
1 tsp panch phoron (page 57)
¼ tsp turmeric powder
2 tsp fennel seeds
¼–½ cup (83–125 ml) sugar
1 tsp sea salt, or to taste

Tomato Sauce with Saffron

Thickened with cashew paste, this sauce goes well with cabbage koftas (page 103), plain paneer cubes (page 42), or fried cheese balls (page 45). You may also add any sautéed, steamed, or roasted vegetables to it. By adding water and adjusting the amount of salt, you can transform this sauce into a soup.

For a lighter version, use homemade yogurt in place of cream.

{MAKES 5–6 CUPS (1.2–1.5 L)}

4–5 medium-size tomatoes
2 tsp coriander seeds
1 tsp jeera seeds
1–2 Tbsp ghee (page 25), butter, or oil
1 cup (125 ml) cashew nuts
½ cup (125 ml) hot water
¾ cup (188 ml) heavy cream
2 cups (250 ml) whey or water
1 tsp cayenne powder
¼ tsp saffron powder
Generous pinch cardamom powder
1½–2 tsp sea salt, or to taste

Wash and peel the tomatoes and cut off the stems. Process them into a paste in an electric spice mill or food processor. Set aside.

Grind the coriander and jeera seeds into a powder with a mortar and pestle or in an electric spice mill.

Heat up the ghee, butter, or oil in a pot. When it's hot but not smoking, add the coriander and jeera powder immediately followed by the tomato paste. Cook, covered, for about 7 minutes or until the tomato paste separates from the fat.

Meanwhile, place the cashews and hot water in an electric spice mill and process until it becomes a smooth paste. Add it to the tomatoes along with the cream and whey (or water). Reduce the heat to moderately low and simmer, covered, for 5 to 6 minutes, then add the cayenne powder, saffron, cardamom, and salt. Turn off the heat and let the flavors steep for 5 minutes.

Quick Eggplant Pickle

The lemon juice and dry mango powder, amchoor, make this is a tangy relish. A spoonful goes a long way. Being oily, it begs to be wrapped in a piece of soft flatbread. I love it with hot, plain rice, too. Thin, long purple eggplants, also known as Japanese eggplants, are best for this recipe. You can simply slice them to get bite-size pieces. If you use regular eggplants, cut them into 2-inch-long (5 cm) and ½-inch-wide (75 mm) sticks.

{MAKES ABOUT 1½ CUPS (375 ML)}

Wash, dry, and thinly slice the eggplants to bite-size pieces. Cut regular eggplants to 2-inch-long (5 cm) and ½-inch-wide (75 mm) sticks. Heat the ghee and oil over moderate heat. When it is hot but not smoking, add the ginger (juice removed) and chilies. When the ginger turns light golden, add the turmeric, cayenne, and hing powder immediately followed by the eggplant. Toss and turn the eggplant with a spatula in the pan to coat it evenly with the spices and add the salt. Cook uncovered for 10 to 15 minutes, occasionally stirring until the vegetables are tender and golden. Keep the temperature throughout the cooking as high as possible without burning the eggplant. Cooking eggplant at lower temperatures may make it soggy.

While the eggplant is cooking, dry roast the coriander and jeera seeds in a skillet or pan over a moderate heat, tossing and turning the spices with a spatula for 5 to 6 minutes, until they are a few shades darker and aromatic. Remove the spices from the heat and let them cool. Grind them into powder and mix it with the lemon juice, sugar, amchoor, and kala namak powder.

When the eggplant is ready, remove it from the heat and add the spiced lemon juice.

Garnish with chopped cilantro before serving. Store in a lidded jar in the refrigerator for not longer than 2 or 3 days.

1 lb (500 g) eggplant
3 Tbsp ghee (page 25)
3 Tbsp sunflower oil
1 Tbsp finely grated ginger (juice removed)
1–2 green chilies, slit
½ tsp turmeric powder
½ tsp cayenne powder
½ tsp hing powder
1½ tsp sea salt, or to taste
2 tsp coriander seeds
2 tsp jeera seeds
3 Tbsp lemon juice
4 Tbsp organic whole cane sugar
2 tsp amchoor powder
1 tsp kala namak powder

TO SERVE
Handful (20 g) of fresh cilantro, chopped

Banana Raita

Naturally sweet and sour, banana raita is a refreshing condiment.
Use firm bananas for an ideal texture.

{SERVES 4}

2 cups (500 ml) homemade
  yogurt (page 34)
1 tsp chaat masala (page 61)
1 mild, red chili pepper
  seeded and minced
½ tsp sea salt, or to taste
2 Tbsp finely grated, fresh
  or desiccated coconut
Handful (20g) of fresh mint
  leaves, chopped
2 bananas

Combine the yogurt in a bowl with all the ingredients, except the
bananas. Whisk until all the ingredients are incorporated. Wash,
peel, and slice the bananas. Fold them into the yogurt. Serve as a
refreshing surprise for a summer lunch or with poories (page 130).

Eggplant Raita

This raita is rich and tangy. Roasted eggplants lend a unique texture to it,
but they can be replaced with any vegetable for variety.

{SERVES 4}

Wash and cut the eggplants into 2-inch-long (5 cm) and ½-inch-wide (75 mm) sticks. If you prefer using thin, Japanese eggplants, slice them into bite-size pieces. Mix them with the ghee or oil, turmeric, cayenne, hing, and salt, and spread them on a baking sheet in a single layer. Bake at 425°F (220°C) for 15 to 20 minutes until they turn dark golden and crisp.

While the eggplants are roasting, whisk the yogurt, crème fraîche, chaat masala, and cilantro in a bowl until smooth. Set the mixture aside.

Dry roast the jeera seeds in a skillet or pan over moderate to moderately low heat, tossing and turning them with a spatula for 5 to 6 minutes until they become a few shades darker and aromatic. Remove the seeds from the heat and let them cool. Grind them into powder.

When the eggplant is ready, combine the pieces with the yogurt. Garnish with jeera powder. Serve warm or cold.

2 eggplants
2–3 Tbsp ghee (page 25) or oil
¼ tsp turmeric powder
¼ tsp cayenne powder
¼ tsp hing powder
½–¾ tsp sea salt, or to taste
2 cups (500 ml) homemade yogurt (page 34)
2 Tbsp homemade crème fraîche (page 33)
2 tsp chaat masala (page 61)
Handful (20 g) of fresh cilantro, chopped
2 tsp jeera seeds

DESSERTS

Bhapa Doi
(Steamed Yogurt Custard) / 200

Pecan and Hazelnut Fudge / 203

Caramel Milk Fudge / 204

Almond Halva / 207

Strawberry Halva / 208

Amrakhand
(Sweet Mango Yogurt) / 211

Kalakand
(Sweet Cheese Confection) / 212

Lemon and Coconut
Sponge Cakes / 215

Melt-in-the-Mouth Candy / 216

Banana and Berry Ice
Cream / 219

Chenna Poda
(Sweet Cheese Pastry) / 220

Lemon and Caramel Tartlets / 222

Berry Soup / 224

Laddu (Chickpea Confection
with Orange Zest) / 227

Fruit and Nut Energy Bars / 228

Gopinath
(Cacao Hazelnut Fudge) / 231

Cherry and Chocolate
Layer Cake / 232

Kheer (Carrot Pudding) / 237

Peach Pie with
Heart-Shaped Crust / 238

Saffron Sandesh / 241

Bhapa Doi
(Steamed Yogurt Custard)

This is my oven-baked version of a classic Bengali delicacy called bhapa doi *(steamed curd).*
You'll expend some effort to make this dessert, but it's time well spent.
Serve it cold as it is or with fresh berries.

{SERVES 4}

2 cups (500 ml) homemade
   yogurt (page 34)
4 cups (1 liter) organic 4% fat
   milk
4 Tbsp cream, 30% fat
Seeds of a vanilla pod
⅓ cup + 1 Tbsp (100 ml)
   refined sugar

Transfer the yogurt to a sieve or colander lined with a large, thin cotton cloth or cheesecloth. If the cloth is too thin, you may want to double the thickness. Otherwise, the cloth will pass through the curd along with the whey. Wrap the cloth around the yogurt and suspend it with string or twine in the refrigerator for 2 to 3 hours or until it has reduced to 1 cup (250 ml) of yogurt. Remember to place a bowl underneath it to collect the whey.

Bring the milk, cream, and vanilla to boil in a thick-bottomed pan or pot over moderate heat. Cook for about 30 minutes, constantly stirring. By now, the milk should have considerably cooked down. Reduce the heat to moderately low and keep stirring while cooking for 10 to 15 minutes more. Stirring is important because it speeds up evaporation and prevents the milk from burning or forming a film on the top. Continue until the milk has reduced by about three-quarters. There should be 1 cup (250 ml) of thick, condensed milk left.

Stir the sugar into the milk. When it has melted, remove the pot from the heat and let it cool for an hour, covered.

Preheat the oven to 350°F (180°C).

In a kettle, boil the water for the water bath. (You will need enough water to reach three-quarters of the way up the sides of the ramekins in the next step.)

Combine the milk and the yogurt in a bowl. Whisk the mixture until it is smooth and pour it into 4 small ramekins. Leave some empty space on the top because the mixture will expand when baked. Place the ramekins in a large ovenproof dish or tray. Fill the dish with boiling water three-quarters up the sides of the ramekins. Be careful not to spill water inside the ramekins!

Bake the pudding for 40 to 50 minutes or up to 1 hour. Cover the ramekins with foil at any point if the pudding seems to be getting too dark on the top.

Remove the ramekins from the oven and carefully lift them from the water bath with the help of a flat spoon or spatula. Cool, cover the ramekins with plastic film, and store them in the refrigerator. The pudding is best eaten the next day.

Pecan and Hazelnut Fudge

Nut-based confections are universal and universally loved, from halva to nougat.
This recipe satisfies the sweet tooth in a jiffy. By using a range of nuts with different textures,
from a paste to a coarse meal, you may adapt this recipe for any occasion or palate.

{MAKES ABOUT 20 TO 25 BITE-SIZE BALLS}

Grind the nuts into powder.

Combine all the ingredients in a heavy-bottomed pan or pot and bring the mixture to a boil over moderate heat. Cook for about 10 minutes, constantly stirring, until the mixture reduces into a thick mass that pulls away from the bottom and sides of the pot. Reduce the heat to moderately low and cook it, vigorously stirring, for 5 to 7 minutes longer or until it becomes a solid, fudge-like mass that is easy to move around the pan. It should look glossy.

Transfer the mixture onto a plate or platter lined with parchment paper. Shape the mixture into a thick rectangle with a spatula. Let it cool to room temperature. Cut the candy into bars or roll it into balls.

For added texture and flavor, roll the balls in or sprinkle the bars with roasted, coarsely chopped nuts. Store refrigerated in a lidded jar for not more than 2 or 3 days.

¼ lb (100 g) pecan nuts
¼ lb (100 g) hazelnuts
1 cup (250 ml) organic milk, 4% fat
1 cup (250 ml) organic whole cane sugar
2 Tbsp unsalted butter or ghee (page 25)
Pinch of salt (optional)
Additional, roasted nuts, to garnish (optional)

Caramel Fudge

This method for making sweets by patiently cooking down a mixture of milk and sugar originates from the town of Mathura, located in the modern state of Uttar Pradesh, where Sri Krishna appeared five thousand years ago. The same fudge-making tradition is carried out today in hundreds of Krishna temples around the world.

These caramel-colored confections are famous for their purity. You may use white or whole cane sugar for making them, and add saffron, cardamom, vanilla, or nuts at the end of cooking. You can also stir in fresh fruit paste for a different taste.

{MAKES 20–25 BITE-SIZE PIECES}

12 cups (3 liters) organic milk, 4% fat
¾–1 cup (188–250 ml) sugar
2 Tbsp unsalted butter

Bring the milk to a boil in a large, heavy-bottomed pan or pot over high heat. As soon as it starts to boil, reduce the heat to moderate and cook, constantly stirring with a wooden spatula, as long as it takes to condense the milk into a thick paste. Scrape the bottom and sides of the pot as the milk boils to prevent scorching and sticking. Be prepared to stand at the stove for over an hour.

When the milk becomes paste-like, add the sugar and butter. Continue cooking, constantly stirring, until it pulls away from the sides and bottom of the pan and forms a solid, fudge-like mass.

Transfer it onto a plate or platter lined with parchment paper. Shape it into a rectangle with a spatula. When it's cool enough to handle, cut it into small squares or roll it into balls. You can use candy molds to decorate the sweets. Store refrigerated in a lidded jar for not more than 2 or 3 days.

Almond Halva

Almond halva has a soft, melt-in-the-mouth texture. Being so mellow, the aroma of this dessert relies on the quality of almonds and saffron. Use the finest choice for both.

{SERVES 4}

Soak the almonds in hot water for at least 10 minutes.

In the meantime, heat 1 tablespoon of the milk in a small pan over high heat. Simultaneously, dry roast the saffron threads on a skillet over moderately low heat for about 30 seconds until they become brittle. Remove the milk from the heat. Rub the saffron into a powder and add it to the milk. Cover and set it aside to infuse.

Slip the almonds out of their skins and use a spice mill or food processor to grind them and ¾ cup (188 ml) of the milk into a smooth paste.

Bring the sugar and water to a boil in a heavy-bottomed pan or pot over high heat. After the sugar has dissolved, reduce the heat to moderately low and add the almond paste. Stir the mixture continually and slowly add the ghee. Continue stirring. After about 15 minutes, the mixture will thicken and become a fudge-like mass that pulls away from the bottom and sides of the pan. At this point, add the saffron milk. Cook 5 minutes longer. Turn off the heat and transfer the mixture to a bowl.

Let the almond halva set for at least 10 minutes before serving. It will further thicken as it cools down. Use an ice cream scoop to spoon out each serving.

⅓ lb (150 g) almonds
¾ cup (188 ml) + 1 Tbsp milk divided
Pinch of saffron threads
½ cup + 2 Tbsp (150 ml) sugar
½ cup + 2 Tbsp (150 ml) water
7 Tbsp melted ghee (page 25) or unsalted butter

Strawberry Halva

Caramelized sugar, strawberries, roasted semolina, and butter unite in this halva. It's especially satisfying when served directly from the stove, piping hot.

Spelt, oat, or wheat semolina can be used, but for a velvety halva the grain must be very fine.

{SERVES 4–6}

4 cups (1 liter) strawberries
¾ cup (188 ml) sugar
1¼ cup (375 ml) whey or
  water
100 g unsalted butter
¾ cup (188 ml/115 g) fine
  semolina
Zest of 1 organic orange

TO SERVE
Cream, vanilla custard,
  or sweet yogurt cheese
  (optional, page 37)

Wash and remove the stems from the strawberries. Set ⅓ of them aside for garnishing and puree the rest either by pressing them through a sieve or using a food processor.

Melt the sugar in a heavy-bottomed pan or pot over moderately high heat. As soon as it melts, reduce the heat to moderate and cook, constantly stirring with a wooden spatula, until it turns light golden and pleasantly fragrant. Add the whey or water. The sugar will momentarily solidify, but keep cooking until it dissolves again. Then reduce the heat, cover the pot, and simmer until needed.

Melt the butter in a large, heavy-bottomed pan or pot over moderate heat. Add the semolina and roast it, constantly stirring with a wooden spatula, for 10 to 12 minutes until it turns golden and aromatic.

Carefully and slowly add the hot syrup into the semolina while using a spatula or spoon with a long handle to stir the mixture to prevent clotting. The semolina will sputter. Be careful and don't burn yourself! Finally, fold in the strawberry puree and orange zest.

Turn off the heat and keep stirring and turning the halva until it thickens and becomes glossy. Serve, preferably warm, and garnish with the rest of the strawberries and cream, vanilla, custard, or sweetened yogurt cheese (optional).

Amrakhand

(Sweet Mango Yogurt)

Shrikhand or strained yogurt is a popular Maharashtrian and Gujarati side dish and dessert.
It's often eaten with poories (page 130).
Amrakhand is simply strained yogurt with mango pulp added.

{SERVES 4}

Heat the milk in a small saucepan or pot over high heat. Simultaneously, dry roast the saffron threads on a skillet over moderately low heat for about 30 seconds until they become brittle. Remove the milk from the heat. Rub the saffron into a powder and add it to the milk. Cover and set it aside to infuse for a couple minutes, then whisk it into the yogurt.

Transfer the curd to a sieve or colander lined with a large, thin cotton cloth or cheesecloth. If the cloth is too thin, you may need to double the thickness. Otherwise, the cloth will pass through the curd along with the whey. Wrap the cloth around the yogurt and suspend it with string or twine in the refrigerator for 6 to 8 hours or until it has reduced to 2 cups (500 ml) of yogurt. Remember to place a bowl underneath to collect the whey.

Wash, peel, deseed, and cut the mango into smaller chunks. Place the mango in a blender or food processor. Run it until the mango turn into a smooth pulp. Add the cream, powdered sugar, and cardamom powder. Pulse a few times until everything is evenly mixed.

Fold the mango pulp into the strained yogurt. Refrigerate and serve it chilled.

Garnish with fresh mango and chopped pistachio nuts.

1 Tbsp milk
Pinch of saffron threads
4 cups (1 liter) homemade
  yogurt (page 34)
1 large, fresh mango
2 Tbsp heavy cream
  (optional)
5–6 Tbsp powdered sugar
¼ tsp cardamom powder

TO SERVE
Fresh mango pieces
  (optional)
Pistachio nuts (optional)

Kalakand

(Sweet Cheese Confection)

The mixture of milk and fresh cheese cooked down into a paste is reminiscent of
the purity and simplicity of old India. Traditionally, kalakand is left grainy because the textures
of solidified milk and cheese offer notable contrast. However, my version is soft and uniform.

{SERVES 4–6}

150 g chenna (fresh cheese)
from 4 cups (1 liter) milk
(see page 42)
¼ cup (63 ml) water
4 cups (1 liter) organic milk,
4% fat
3–4 Tbsp sugar
1 Tbsp ghee (page 25) or
unsalted butter
Pistachio nuts, to garnish

Make the fresh cheese from 4 cups (1 liter) of milk according to the instructions on page 42 and transfer it to a sieve or colander lined with a large cotton cloth and hang it over the sink for not longer than 10 minutes.

While you are making the cheese, heat the water in a separate, heavy-bottomed pan over high heat. When it's boiling, add the milk and bring it to a boil over moderate temperature. Keep stirring and mixing the milk after it begins to boil to prevent scorching. Cook it until it has reduced to half the original volume. Remember to stir the milk regularly.

After hanging it for 10 minutes, unwrap the cheese and place it in a food processor. Run the processor until the cheese is soft and without a touch of graininess. In the absence of a food processor, knead the cheese with your palm against the clean kitchen counter until it is smooth.

When the milk has reduced by half, add the cheese. From here on, constantly stir the mixture.

When it turns into a thick paste and pulls away from the bottom and sides of the pan, reduce the heat to moderately low and add the sugar. Keep stirring until it thickens to the point that it forms a solid, fudge-like mass. By now, the milk has been cooking down for about 50 to 60 minutes.

Add the ghee or butter, and stir for 5 minutes more. It should look glossy. The consistency should be such that it holds together but spreads down very slowly when you collect the fudge into a pile.

Transfer the mixture to a buttered tray or platter. Pat it into a thick rectangle, garnish it with nuts, and set it aside to cool.

Before serving, cut the sweet into bite-size squares. Store refrigerated in a lidded jar for not more than 2 or 3 days.

Lemon and Coconut Sponge Cakes

These dairy-free sponge cakes have a tangy edge. They are sweet, moist, refreshing, and irresistible!

{MAKES ONE 5 × 5 INCH (25 × 25 CM) SQUARE CAKE
OR 5-INCH (25 CM) ROUND CAKE}

Preheat the oven to 300°F (150°C).

Combine the cake flour, coconut flour, baking powder, baking soda, salt, and sugar in a bowl. Set the dry ingredients aside.

Wash, crack open, and peel the brown skin from the coconut. Reserve the coconut water. Place the coconut meat in a blender with the hot water. Process the mixture until it turns into a smooth paste. Press the coconut milk through a sieve into a bowl. Cool it down by placing the bowl inside a bigger bowl filled with ice-cold water. Transfer the coconut meat to a baking tray and lightly toast it for about 10 minutes until it becomes dry and aromatic. Set it aside.

When the coconut milk reaches room temperature, add the oil, lemon juice and zest, and the flaxseed powder to it. Then, carefully fold the wet ingredients into the dry ones. Don't overmix! The consistency should be thicker than that of a regular cake batter. You may need to add a few spoonsful of water if it's too dry.

Transfer the batter to a rectangular loaf pan or a cake form lined with a baking sheet. Smooth the surface with a spatula. Bake it in the lower third of the oven for 30 to 40 minutes or up to 1 hour, until a toothpick comes out clean when inserted. Remove the cake from the oven and turn it upside down on a wire rack.

While the cake is baking, melt the sugar in a pot or pan over high heat. Shake the pan to ensure it melts evenly. As soon as it turns light golden, add the lemon juice. It will foam and sputter for a moment. Reduce the heat to low and simmer for 5 to 10 minutes until the sugar has melted again. Add the coconut oil and keep simmering for another 5 minutes. Remove the pan from the heat and spoon the sauce evenly on all sides of the cake while it is cooling on the wire rack. It's a good idea to place a tray underneath the rack. The cake should absorb all of the syrup.

Cut the cake into serving-size slices and roll each in the lightly toasted coconut.

FOR THE CAKE
1 cup (250 ml) spelt cake flour
½ cup (125 ml) coconut flour
1 tsp baking powder
½ tsp baking soda
Pinch of salt
½ cup (125 ml) sugar
1 coconut
1¼ cup (313 ml) boiling water
4 Tbsp coconut oil
2 Tbsp lemon juice
Zest of 2 organic lemons
1 Tbsp ground flaxseeds

FOR THE SYRUP
1 cup (250 ml) sugar
½ cup (125 ml) lemon juice
1 Tbsp organic cold-pressed
    coconut oil (or butter)

Melt-in-the-Mouth Candy

Made of generous amounts of ghee and sugar syrup, this rich, mouthwatering fudge is not for the fainthearted. It's known as Mysore Pak, the royal sweet of the Karnataka region of India.

{MAKES ABOUT 20–25 PIECES}

1 cup (250 ml) + 2 Tbsp ghee
  (page 25), divided
⅔ cup (167 ml) chickpea flour
1⅓ cup (333 ml) sugar,
  or to taste
1 cup (250 ml) water
Pinch of cardamom powder

Line a plate or platter with a sheet of baking paper and set it aside.

Melt 1 cup (250 ml) of the ghee in a small pot over high heat; when it is hot but not smoking, reduce the heat to moderately low. Keep a ladle next to it.

Dry roast the chickpea flour on a skillet or pan over moderate heat for 4 or 5 minutes, constantly stirring, until it turns a few shades darker and aromatic. Transfer it to a bowl. Rub 2 tablespoons of melted ghee into the flour with your hand until it resembles bread crumbs. Now press it through a sieve to remove any lumps and set it aside.

Heat the sugar and water in a large, heavy-bottomed pan or pot over moderate heat. Cook it for 10 to 12 minutes or until it forms a distinct consistency: there should be a single thread of syrup when you pull apart a drop of boiling sugar between your thumb and middle finger. You can also test it by dropping a little bit of syrup into a cup of ice-cold water. It should immediately crystallize.

When the sugar has reached the proper consistency, gradually add the chickpea flour to it while whisking the mixture to prevent clotting. Finally, add the cardamom powder.

Now, reduce the heat to moderately low.

Stir a ladleful of ghee into the chickpea flour paste. It will froth up and bubble! Use a whisk, ladle, or spatula with a long handle to mix it. When the ghee has absorbed, pour in another ladleful. Stir and keep adding ghee until the paste becomes a silky thick batter with a golden hue.

Stir the mixture until it pulls away from the sides and bottom of the pan and becomes aromatic. As soon as it forms a solid, fudge-like mass that is easy to move around the pan, remove it from the heat and transfer it to a plate or platter lined with a sheet of parchment paper. Smooth the surface with a rubber spatula.

Let the mixture cool, then cut it into squares. Because of the high ghee content, it will store well at room temperature for weeks.

Banana and Berry Ice Cream

Bananas become creamy when frozen and pureed. Combined with berries, fruits, nuts, cacao, caramel, or other flavors, they turn into soft ice cream that is light and delicious. The recipe is easy to make dairy-free by substituting yogurt with coconut milk or fruit juices or omitting the liquid.

If you are less fond of the taste of banana and want to hide it, add berries that have a strong flavor, like raspberries or strawberries.

{SERVES 4}

Wash, peel, and slice the bananas. Place them in a zip-top bag and freeze them overnight. Wash, pit, and freeze the fruits or berries the same way.

When you are ready to make the ice cream, combine the frozen bananas and fruits or berries in a food processor. Run the processor until the mixture turns into a crumble. Add the sugar and yogurt. Process it until the mixture has the texture of soft ice cream. At the very end, add the lemon juice. Serve the ice cream immediately or freeze it until it reaches a desired consistency.

6–7 ripe bananas

4 cups (1 liter) fresh fruits or berries

5 Tbsp organic whole cane sugar or to taste

3 Tbsp homemade yogurt

4–5 Tbsp lemon juice or to taste

Chenna Poda

(Sweet Cheese Pastry)

This signature dessert is from the state of Odisha. It's a cheesecake originally baked over an earthen fire for hours until "the cheese burns"—that's how chenna poda translates from Odia dialect. According to hearsay, the delicacy came about by accident when a sweets maker noticed that a mixture of fresh cheese and date molasses, gur, he had forgotton on the fire overnight had turned into a luscious cake. Like many other kitchen mishaps, chenna poda became a part of culture. Today it is available around India.

It's said to be the favorite sweet of Sri Jagannath, the deity worshipped at the temple of Puri along with his brother, Balaram, and sister, Subhadra. Once a year they are brought out in the streets in three massive chariots so that those who don't come to the temple may also see their smiling faces.

I have added orange zest to the traditional recipe.

{MAKES 12 CUPCAKE-SIZE SWEETS}

450 g chenna (fresh cheese)
  (page 42)
4 Tbsp fine semolina
¾ cup + 1 Tbsp (200 ml)
  sugar
½ tsp cardamom powder
Zest of 2 organic oranges

FOR THE CARAMEL
5 Tbsp sugar
¼ cup (63 ml) water
Melted ghee (page 25) or
  butter

Preheat the oven to 350°F (180°C).

Cream the cheese in the food processor. Alternatively, you can knead it with your palm until it is smooth and without a touch of graininess.

Mix the cheese, semolina, sugar, cardamom powder, and orange zest in a bowl by hand until the mixture is smooth. Set it aside.

Melt the sugar for the caramel in a pot or pan over high heat. Shake the pan to ensure it melts evenly. As soon as it turns golden, add the water. When it bubbles, turn off the heat.

Brush the cupcake tins liberally with melted ghee or butter. Pour a little bit of caramel into each tin and spread it evenly in the bottom. Use a pastry bag to pipe the cheese mixture on the top.

Cover the cupcake tins with foil and bake the cakes for 20 to 30 minutes or until a toothpick comes out clean when inserted. Remove the cakes from the oven.

Let the cakes cool, covered, before turning the forms upside down. Chenna poda is best served warm as an after-lunch treat or with a cup of herbal tea. Consider pairing the cakes with a simple berry sauce or jam, too.

Lemon and Caramel Tartlets

These tartlets are filled with quick-to-make lemon fudge. The measurement given for the milk powder may vary according to its absorbency. You may need less if the milk powder is coarse, and more if it is superfine. The filling should be the consistency of thick cake batter that holds its shape for piping.

{MAKES EIGHT 3½-INCH (9 CM) TARTLETS
OR ONE 8- TO 10-INCH (20–25 CM) TART}

FOR THE TART CRUST
1 cup (250 ml) organic
   all-purpose spelt flour
½ tsp sea salt
1 Tbsp sugar
6 Tbsp (75 g) unsalted butter
2–4 Tbsp cold cream
   (heavy or light)

FOR THE FILLING
½ cup (125 ml) sugar
10 Tbsp (125 g) unsalted
   butter
Finely grated zest of 2
   organic lemons
1¼ cup (313 ml) organic milk,
   4% fat
1¼ cup (313 ml) milk powder,
   or as needed
4 Tbsp lemon juice

TO SERVE
Fresh berries

Mix the flour, salt, and sugar in a bowl. Rub in the butter with your fingertips or a fork until the mixture resembles a coarse crumble. Add the cream. Quickly gather the dough into a ball. You may need to add a few drops of cream or a sprinkle of flour to reach the right consistency. The exact amount of liquid depends on the absorbency of the flour. The dough should hold together but still be crumbly. Avoid kneading it too much.

Wrap the dough with plastic wrap and shape it into a disk. Refrigerate it for at least 30 minutes or until you are ready to bake it.

Preheat the oven to 350°F (180°C).

Unwrap the dough. Sandwich it between two sheets of parchment paper or plastic wrap and roll it into a thin disk. Remove the top layer of paper or plastic wrap and cut out rounds of dough that are slightly larger than the tart forms you are using. Press them on the bottom and sides of the form and trim the edges. Alternatively, you can make one large tart. Prick the bottom crust with a fork in several places.

Bake the tarts in the lower third of the oven for 12 to 15 minutes until the crust is a light golden color. Cool them completely before filling them.

Melt the sugar in a pot or pan over high heat. As soon as it melts, reduce the heat to moderate. Shake the pan to melt the sugar evenly. As soon as it turns golden, add the butter and lemon zest. Cook the mixture until the butter melts. Add the milk and bring it to a boil. Cook for 12 minutes, constantly stirring with a wooden spoon. The milk should become reduced and thick. Remove it from the heat and discard the pieces of lemon zest by pouring the milk through a sieve into a bowl. You should have 1 cup (250 ml) of condensed milk. Plunge the bowl in cold water to cool down the milk.

When the condensed milk reaches room temperature, add the milk powder. Whisk the mixture until it is smooth. You may want to use an immersion blender. Finally, blend in the lemon juice. Spoon or pipe the filling carefully into the tart crusts. Level the surfaces with a pastry knife.

Store the tarts in the refrigerator and garnish with fresh berries just before serving.

Berry Soup

*Berry soup is a delightful dessert or a small meal. When the harvest is abundant,
in the summer and autumn, it is as healthy as it is vibrant.*

For special occasions, layer it with whipped cream or vanilla custard.

{SERVES 4 TO 6}

2 cups (500 ml) raspberries
1 vanilla bean
4 cups (1 liter) water
¾ cup (188 ml) sugar, or to
taste
3 Tbsp potato starch
3 Tbsp cold water

TO SERVE
4 cups (1 liter) mixed, fresh
berries

Wash the raspberries, press them through a sieve, and discard the seeds. Set the puree aside.

Scrape out the seeds from the vanilla bean and place them, along with the empty bean pod, raspberry puree, water, and sugar in a pan or pot. Bring the mixture to a boil over moderate heat. As soon as it boils, reduce the heat to moderately low and cook 2 to 3 minutes. Then remove it from the heat and discard the vanilla bean.

Mix the potato starch and cold water in a small bowl or cup until it's smooth. Pour it in a continuous stream into the boiled raspberry syrup while stirring with a spoon or spatula.

Return the mixture to the heat. As soon as it bubbles once and thickens, remove it from the heat. Add the berries and serve hot.

If you want to serve it cool, do not add the berries. Cover the surface with plastic wrap before letting it cool. Otherwise a skin will form on the top. Remove the wrap and top with the berries just before serving.

Laddu

(Chickpea Confection with Orange Zest)

This recipe shows the versatility of legumes. Chickpea flour plays the main role.
Orange zest gives it a light, fresh accent, and almonds offer crunchiness.

{MAKES 20 TO 25 PIECES}

Melt the butter in a heavy-bottomed pan or pot over moderate heat. When it melts, add the coconut oil and then vigorously whisk in the chickpea flour to prevent it from forming lumps. Roast the flour for 6 to 7 minutes, constantly stirring with a wooden spatula, until it turns golden and aromatic. Add the almond slivers and fry them 1 to 2 minutes. Remove the pan from the heat and let the mixture cool for 10 minutes.

Whisk in the milk powder and orange zest. Finally, add the honey. Mix well.

Spread the mixture in a container or platter lined with parchment paper. When the mixture is cool enough to handle, roll it into balls or cut it into squares.

Store the confection in an airtight container, refrigerated for not longer than 2 or 3 days.

8 Tbsp (120 g) unsalted butter
1–2 Tbsp organic cold-pressed coconut oil
1 cup (250 ml) chickpea flour
2 Tbsp almond slivers
1 Tbsp milk powder
2 tsp finely grated orange zest
4 Tbsp honey

Fruit and Nut Energy Bars

Instead of munching dry fruits and nuts to push up the blood sugar level between meals, blend them into delicious energy bars. You can use any ingredients available and make unlimited variations per your taste. This is my current favorite combination.

{MAKES 8 BARS}

1¼ cups (313 ml) almonds
1¼ cups (313 ml) dry pineapple chunks
4 Tbsp cacao or carob powder
3 Tbsp cold-pressed organic coconut oil
2 Tbsp organic whole cane sugar
Pinch of sea or Himalaya salt
Zest of 2 organic oranges
1 Tbsp orange juice
1 Tbsp lemon juice
Desiccated coconut, for garnishing (optional)

You can use the almonds raw or roasted. If roasting, place them on a baking sheet in a preheated oven at 350°F (180°C) and roast them, occasionally tossing, until they are golden on all sides. Let them cool before grinding them.

Place the almonds in an electric spice mill. Pulse them until they are a fine powder. Transfer them to a food processor and add the pineapple chunks. Process until minced.

Add the cacao powder, coconut oil, whole cane sugar, salt, orange zest, and juices. Blend until the ingredients are fully incorporated and form a solid mass.

Transfer the mixture onto a working surface lined with parchment paper. Place another sheet of parchment on top of it and roll it into a thick rectangle. Remove the papers and divide the mixture into small logs.

Place the desiccated coconut on a plate or platter. Roll each log in coconut.

Serve immediately, or cover and refrigerate.

Gopinath
(Cacao Hazelnut Fudge)

I learned this recipe years ago when I lived in the temple ashram. Gopinath is one of Krishna's names, meaning the consort of cowherd girls. Bhakti yoga tradition is so personal that we even name what we eat after our object of meditation in order to stay focused in all circumstances—even when honoring sweet treats!

In most temples chocolate is considered impure because it contains theobromine. Like all stimulants, it is unfavorable for yogic practices that require concentration and clarity of thought. Therefore, Gopinath is made with carob powder, which has hardly a trace amount of theobromine. You can try using cacao one time and carob powder another, and see if your body reacts differently to them.

{ M A K E S   20   T O   25   P I E C E S }

Roast the hazelnuts in the oven at 300°F (150°C) until the skins crackle. Remove the skins and chop the nuts coarsely. Set them aside.

Melt the butter and coconut oil in a heavy-bottomed pan or pot over moderate heat. Remove the pan from the heat and let the butter and oil cool for 15 minutes until its temperature is 100°F (37°C) or lower.

Pour the cacao or carob powder through a sieve and into the butter-oil mixture. Use a whisk or electric hand mixer to break apart the lumps.

Beat the cream in a separate bowl until it forms soft peaks. Whisk in the vanilla seeds and powder sugar. Fold the butter-oil-carob mixture into the cream, then the milk powder, and finally the hazelnuts.

Transfer the fudge into a 4- to 5-inch (20–25 cm) container lined with parchment paper. Refrigerate and cut the fudge into bite-size squares before serving. Alternatively, you can spoon the fudge into paper candy cups or cupcake liners, and refrigerate them before serving.

Because of the low melting point of coconut oil, this sweet must be served cold. Store it in the refrigerator in an airtight container for not longer than 2 to 3 days.

¼ cup (63 ml) hazelnuts

4 Tbsp (50 g) unsalted butter

¼ cup (63 ml) coconut butter or oil

5 Tbsp cacao or carob powder

¾ cup + 1 Tbsp (200 ml) heavy cream

Seeds of 1 vanilla pod

1 cup (250 ml) powdered sugar

1 cup + 4 Tbsp (300 ml) milk powder, or as needed

Cherry and Chocolate Layer Cake

The recipe makes an 8-inch (20 cm) cake with three layers or a 6-inch (15 cm) cake with five layers.
It's composed of dark notes of chocolate and cherries and is pleasantly not-too-sweet.
When baking cakes, always use flour milled especially for cake.
Cake flour utilizes the innermost parts of the grain and, therefore, has the lowest amount of gluten.
Low-gluten flour yields softer, fluffier results.
I find extra-fine spelt best for making soft sponge cakes.

{MAKES ONE 8-INCH (20 CM) CAKE OR ONE 6-INCH (15 CM) CAKE}

FOR THE CAKE
6 Tbsp (80 g) unsalted butter,
  melted
6 Tbsp dark cocoa powder
1 cup (250 ml) powder sugar
4 Tbsp orange juice
1½ cup (375 ml) cultured buttermilk (or yogurt +
  1 tsp lemon juice)
2–2½ cups (500–650 ml) cake
  flour (spelt or wheat)
¼ tsp sea salt
2 tsp baking soda

FOR THE CHERRY SAUCE
1 Tbsp lemon juice
⅓ cup (83 ml) organic whole
  cane sugar
1 cup (250 ml) pitted and halved
  fresh cherries

FOR THE FROSTING
450 g fresh cheese (chenna)
  (page 42)
5 Tbsp organic coconut oil
1 cup (250 ml) powder sugar
Seeds of a vanilla bean
1 tsp beet juice (for color),
  or as needed (see note)
1 cup (250 ml) heavy cream
2 cups (500 ml) pitted and
  halved fresh cherries

FOR THE CARAMEL SAUCE
1 cup (250 ml) heavy cream
1 cup (250 ml) organic whole
  cane sugar
1 Tbsp unsalted butter
Pinch of salt

NOTE: To make beet juice,
  finely grate a small beet and
  squeeze the juice out of it.

/ Continued /

Preheat the oven to 300°F (150°C).

Mix the melted butter, cocoa powder, sugar, and orange juice in a bowl. Whisk the mixture until it is smooth. Add the buttermilk or yogurt-lemon mixture.

In another bowl, combine the flour, sea salt, and baking soda. Use a sieve to add it gradually to the bowl of wet ingredients and gently fold it in with a rubber spatula. Stir the batter as little as necessary to make it smooth. Avoid overworking the batter because it will change the texture of the cake. The exact amount of flour depends on its absorbency. You may not need to add as much as the recipe suggests.

Pour the batter into a cake form lined with parchment paper. Bake it in the lower third of the oven for 50 to 70 minutes until a toothpick comes out clean when inserted. Let the cake cool for 15 minutes before turning it upside down and removing the form.

While the cake is cooling, make the sauce for moistening the cake. Combine the lemon juice, sugar, and cherries in the blender and process the mixture until it is smooth. Pour the mixture through a sieve and discard the cherry skins.

Make the frosting by processing the cheese in the food processor until it's silky and without any touch of graininess. Combine it with the coconut oil, powdered sugar, vanilla seeds, and beet juice in a bowl. The beet juice gives it a pink color.

In a separate bowl, whip the cream until it forms stiff peaks. Fold it carefully into the cheese mixture. Transfer the frosting into a pastry bag.

When the cake is completely cool, cut it into layers. Place the first layer back into a washed and dried baking pan and brush it with the sauce. Add a handful of cherries on the top and cover them with the frosting. Repeat this process with the rest of the layers. Cover the cake with a plate or plastic wrap and place it in the refrigerator for at least 6 hours or overnight.

About 15 to 20 minutes before you are ready to serve the cake, unwrap it and place it on a cake stand or plate.

Make the caramel sauce by bringing the cream and sugar to a boil in a heavy-bottomed pan or pot over moderate heat. Cook it, constantly stirring with a wooden spoon, for 10 to 15 minutes until the caramel thickens. To test its readiness, drop a little bit into a glass of ice-cold water. It should sink to the bottom and solidify immediately. At this stage, fold in the butter and salt. As soon as the butter melts, pour the sauce over the top of the cake. Extra frosting and caramel sauce will keep in the refrigerator for 1 to 2 days.

Kheer

(Carrot Pudding)

Rich, sweet, and visually stunning, this carrot pudding, also known as kheer, is a dessert to make in advance—and in great quantity. You can spoon or slurp it directly from a glass hot, warm, or cold.

{SERVES 4}

Bring the milk to a boil in a large, heavy-bottomed pan or pot over high heat. As soon as it starts to boil, reduce the heat to moderate and cook, constantly stirring with a wooden spatula, until it reduces by one-quarter. When you have about 4 cups (1 liter) of milk left, reduce the heat to minimum.

Heat the ghee or butter in a pan or pot over moderate heat and add the grated carrots. Fry them for 5 to 6 minutes until they become somewhat tender and bright orange. Add 2 ladlesful of hot milk to it and cook, constantly stirring, for 5 to 6 minutes until the carrots are buttery soft. Now, remove the pan from the heat and puree the carrots in a blender or spice mill. Press the paste through a sieve into the milk that is still in another pot.

Add the sugar into the milk and bring it back to a boil over moderate heat. Cook it gently, occasionally stirring, for 5 minutes.

While cooking the milk, dry roast the saffron threads on a skillet over moderately low heat for about 30 seconds until they become brittle. Remove the skillet from the heat and rub the saffron into a powder. Add it, along with the cardamom, to the carrot milk. Simmer for another 5 minutes. The consistency should be like that of thick cream. Remove from the heat.

Garnish the pudding with roasted almond slivers before serving.

6 cups (1.5 liter) organic milk 4% fat
2 Tbsp ghee (page 25) or unsalted butter
1 cup (250 ml) finely grated carrots
⅓–½ cup (83–125 ml) sugar
Generous pinch of saffron threads
Pinch of cardamom powder

TO SERVE
Roasted, slivered almonds, to garnish

Peach Pie with Heart-Shaped Crust

Pie's perfection lies in its imperfection. It's the creative crust and spilled juices that appeal to our senses. Instead of peaches, try apricots, cherries, nectarines, plums, or any combination of seasonal fruit.

{MAKES ONE 8 × 10 INCH (20–25 CM) PIE}

FOR THE CRUST
¼ cup (63 ml) wholegrain
  spelt flour
1 cup (250 ml) all-purpose
  spelt flour
1 Tbsp sugar
½ tsp sea salt
¼ lb (120 g) cold unsalted
  butter
¼ cup (63 ml) ice-cold water,
  or as needed

FOR THE FILLING
12 cups (3 liters) boiling water
  for scalding
3½ lbs (1.5 kg) peaches
2 Tbsp lemon juice
¾ cup (188 ml) sugar
¼ tsp cinnamon powder
Pinch of nutmeg powder
Pinch of salt
3 Tbsp corn starch
Milk or water, for brushing
Sugar for sprinkling on the
  top

Make the dough by mixing the flours, sugar, and salt in a bowl. Cut the butter into small cubes and cut it into the flour with a fork until the mixture resembles a coarse crumble with visible (pea-size) pearls of butter. Add the water gradually while pulling the dough into a rough ball with a spatula. You may need more or less water, depending on the absorbency of the flour.

Divide the dough into two parts and wrap each in plastic wrap. Flatten them slightly and place them in the refrigerator to rest for at least 20 minutes.

Meanwhile, bring the water to boil for scalding the peaches. Wash the peaches and cut a shallow cross at the top of each. Plunge the peaches in a pot of boiling water for 1 minute. Drain and rinse them with cold water. Slip the skins off with the help of a paring knife. Pit and slice them. Set them aside.

Preheat the oven to 400°F (200°C).

Unwrap a portion of the dough. Roll it into a thin round between two sheets of parchment paper sprinkled with flour. It should be big enough to cover the bottom and sides of an 8 to 10-inch (20–25 cm) pie pan. Remove the top sheet and transfer the crust to the form. Peel away the second piece of parchment. Trim the edges. Put it back in the refrigerator while you roll out the top crust.

Unwrap the second portion of dough and roll it, similarly, into a thin disk. Use a cookie cutter to cut small heart shapes from it. Alternatively, you may use it as such (pierced with a knife) or make a lattice top for the pie.

Combine the peaches, lemon juice, sugar, spices, salt, and corn starch. Take out the pie pan and pour the filling in it. Cover it with the heart-shaped pieces of crust and brush it with milk or water. Sprinkle the top with sugar and bake the pie in the bottom third of the oven for about 50 minutes. If the edges are becoming too dark, cover them with a piece of foil.

Serve hot or cold. The filling thickens as it cools for easier serving.

Saffron Sandesh

Sandesh is perhaps the most famous Bengali sweetmeat. It is made by heating fresh cheese and sugar on a low flame, which takes practice to perfect. I am introducing here a simpler method that is easy even for beginners. If you serve sandesh as part of a larger menu with several other desserts, always guide your guests to start with sandesh. Its sweetness is like a whisper that easily becomes crushed under louder and sharper voices.

{MAKES 15 TO 20 PIECES}

Make the fresh cheese as instructed on page 42, and press it under a weight no longer than 7 minutes. Unwrap and transfer it to a food processor.

Dry roast the saffron threads on a skillet over moderately low heat for about 30 seconds until they become brittle. Remove the skillet from the heat and rub the saffron with your hands until it turns to powder. Heat the milk in a small cup or pot and add the saffron powder to it.

Pour the saffron milk on the top of the cheese. Process until the cheese becomes smooth and without a touch of graininess. It will become a solid ball when the processing is done. Transfer it to a bowl.

Knead in the powdered sugar. The ratio is either 1 part sugar and 3 parts cheese or 1 part sugar and 4 parts cheese. Adjust the ratio according to your taste.

Divide the cheese into equal-size portions. Roll each one into a smooth ball. If you rub a little bit of ghee in your hands, the cheese won't stick to them. You can use candy molds to decorate the sweets.

This "instant" sandesh is best eaten during the day it's prepared. If you must, store it in an airtight container and refrigerate it at most for 2 days.

450 g fresh cheese (chenna) (page 42)
Pinch of saffron threads
⅛ tsp milk
1 cup (250 ml) powdered sugar, or to taste

DRINKS

Lime and Cucumber Drink / 244

Pomegranate Juice / 245

Beet and Carrot Juice / 246

Savory Green Smoothie / 247

Strawberry Lassi / 248

Savory Lassi / 249

Golden Milk / 250

Warm Apple Cider / 251

Yogi Tea / 252

Lime and Cucumber Drink

I hope this flavored water inspires you to drink more throughout the day.
Sip it 30 minutes before or 2 hours after each meal as a refreshment.

{MAKES 8 CUPS (2 LITERS)}

2 organic lemons or limes
½ organic cucumber
8 cups (2 liters) water
Handful (20 g) of fresh mint
  leaves

Wash the lemons or limes and cucumber thoroughly. Slice them and combine with the water and mint leaves in a bowl or jar. Cover and let the flavors infuse overnight in the refrigerator. Bring the drink to room temperature and strain it before serving. Garnish with fresh mint leaves.

Pomegranate Juice

Pomegranate is a sweet fruit with astringent notes. It has been used for traditional remedies
for thousands of years. The juice is considered a tonic for the heart and throat.
It counterbalances a diet high in sweet and fatty elements.

{MAKES ABOUT 3 CUPS (750 ML)}

Select heavy and ripe pomegranates.

Wash the pomegranates. Quarter them by cutting four shallow slits through the outer rinds and pulling the sections apart over a large bowl. Scrape the seeds out with your hands. Squeeze out as much juice as possible. Finally, press the seeds through a sieve to extract the rest of the juice. Discard the seeds and pith.

Combine the pomegranate juice and lemon, sugar, and water. Pomegranate juice is a great way to start a day before breakfast.

4½ lbs (2 kg) pomegranates
2 Tbsp lemon juice
2–3 Tbsp organic whole cane sugar
2 cups (500 ml) cold water

Beet and Carrot Juice

This drink is full of antioxidants, minerals, and vitamins.
It purifies and distributes a good kind of energy throughout the body.
It is the go-to juice if you feel exhausted between meals or you want to boost an athletic performance.

{SERVES 2}

1 lb (500 g) beets
2 carrots
5 oranges
1 lemon

TO SERVE
Pinch of kala namak

Wash, peel, and finely grate the beets and carrots. Squeeze out the juice by hand through a sieve. You may want to use vinyl gloves because the juices may stain your skin. Set aside the juice and reserve the pulp. You can use the vegetable pulp for making patties or koftas (page 99) later.

Wash the oranges and lemon. Press the juice out of them and mix it with the beet juice. Add a pinch of kala namak before serving.

Savory Green Smoothie

I consider green smoothies to be liquid salads. They are nutritionally packed and easy to digest.

Basically you can blend any nuts, vegetables, and herbs into a drink, but you need to have a powerful appliance, such as a Vitamix, to do the job. If you have a sensitive digestive system, don't mix fruits (with the exception of lemons) or berries with vegetables; it would likely cause flatulence or other stomach maladies.

{MAKES 6 CUPS (1.5 LITERS)}

Place the ingredients in a blender and process them until the mixture is smooth. Adjust the amount of water, spices, and salt to your taste.

¼ lb (100 g) assorted nuts (such as almonds, cashews, sunflower seeds, sesame seeds)
4 cups (1 liter) water
Generous handful of baby spinach
2 cups (500 ml) coarsely chopped lettuce or mixed salad greens
1–2 avocados, pitted and peeled
1–2 small cucumbers, cut in chunks
2 handfuls of fresh basil
Juice of 1 lime
Juice of 2–3 lemons
½ tsp dry-roasted jeera
½ tsp freshly ground black pepper
½ tsp kala namak powder
½ tsp cayenne powder
1½ tsp sea salt, or to taste
1 Tbsp extra virgin olive oil

Strawberry Lassi

Pink and speckled with vanilla seeds, strawberry lassi is as refreshing as it is pretty to look at.
The secret of the recipe lies in the homemade dairy. It makes all the difference.
Organic whole cane sugar gives an earthy, natural sweetness.

{MAKES 4 CUPS (1 LITER)}

4 cups (1 liter) fresh strawberries
Half of 1 vanilla bean
1½ cup (375 ml) homemade
  yogurt or cultured buttermilk
1½ cup (375 ml) water
6 Tbsp organic whole cane
  sugar, or to taste

Wash and clean the strawberries. Place them in a blender or food processor. Scrape out the seeds of the vanilla bean half, and combine them, along with the rest of the ingredients, with the strawberries. Discard the bean. Process until the drink is mixed and smooth. Serve immediately or as one of the drinks for a festive meal.

Savory Lassi

Seasoned lassi is an excellent cooling beverage for hot summer days. It increases appetite and aids digestion. Yogurt's probiotic properties improve the intestinal flora.

For higher nutritional value and balance, use Himalayan salt instead of sea salt.

{MAKES 4 CUPS (I LITER)}

Dry roast the jeera seeds on a skillet or pan over moderate to moderately low heat, tossing and turning them with a spatula for 5 to 6 minutes until the seeds become a few shades darker and aromatic. Remove them from the heat and let them cool. Grind them into coarse powder.

Combine all the ingredients and mix well.

½–1 tsp jeera seeds
4 cups (1 liter) takra (page 38)
¼ tsp turmeric powder
Pinch of hing
½ tsp kala namak
¼ tsp Himalaya salt, or to taste

Golden Milk

According to ayurveda, milk increases strength, immunity, happiness, and contentment.
Drinking a cup of gently boiled milk in the evening calms the body and mind and helps to prepare for the night.
Spices reduce the body's propensity to create mucus, and ghee lubricates the joints.

{MAKES 4 CUPS (1 LITER)}

4 cups (1 liter) organic milk, 4% fat

2 tsp ghee (page 25)

1 Tbsp fresh, grated ginger

2 tsp fresh, grated turmeric or 1 tsp turmeric powder

3" (7.5 cm) piece of cinnamon stick

1 tsp whole black peppercorns

Generous pinch of powdered nutmeg (optional)

5 Tbsp organic whole cane sugar, or to taste

Combine the ingredients in a pan or pot over moderate heat. Bring the mixture to a boil, turn off the heat, cover, and let the flavors steep for 5 to 7 minutes. Then, strain the milk. Serve immediately.

Warm Apple Cider

Hot cider is an ideal beverage for the autumn and winter seasons.
The aroma alone inspires a good mood!

{MAKES 10 CUPS (2.5 LITERS)}

Wash the apples, orange, and lemon. Slice the fruit and combine them with the water, cloves, cardamoms, cinnamon sticks, and a pinch of nutmeg in a pot. Slit the vanilla bean open and scrape out the seeds. Add them and the empty pod to the pot. Bring the pot to a boil over high heat. Then, reduce the heat to low and simmer for 30 minutes. Remove the pot from the heat and strain the liquid through a sieve. If you don't mind a thicker, opaque drink, press the apples through the sieve, too. Finally, add the sugar. Mix and serve warm.

5 organic apples
1 organic orange
1 organic lemon
8 cups (2 liters) water
2 cloves
2 cardamom pods, crushed
2 cinnamon sticks
Pinch of nutmeg
1 vanilla bean
½ cup (125 ml) organic whole
   cane sugar

Yogi Tea

This brew is full of soothing ingredients. It's a blend of sweet and warming spices.

{MAKES 4 CUPS (1 LITER)}

4 cups (1 liter) water
3" (7 cm) piece of licorice
  root or ½ tsp licorice
  powder
½ tsp dry ginger powder or
  2 tsp grated fresh ginger
  root
¼ tsp ground cinnamon
¼ tsp freshly ground black
  pepper
Pinch each of cardamom,
  cloves, and cayenne pepper
½ cup (125 ml) milk
Honey, to taste (optional)

Combine all of the ingredients except the milk and honey in a pot. Bring the liquid to a boil over high heat. Immediately reduce the heat to low and simmer, covered, for 5 minutes. Then, remove the pan from heat, discard the licorice stick (if using whole), and add the milk. Serve immediately. If you like to sweeten the tea, add honey to your taste into each cup.

part
Two

MY INGREDIENTS
& KITCHEN TOOLS

INGREDIENTS

Dairy

I use organic cow milk that has around 4% fat in all of the recipes of the book. It's the best quality milk available here in Finland at the moment. It's pasteurized but not homogenized.

Pasteurization refers to a brief heating of raw milk in order to kill harmful microorganisms. As a side effect, vitamin and mineral content is somewhat reduced. Homogenization, on the other hand, alludes to mechanically forcing milk through small pipes at high pressure, during which the fat globules reduce in size and distribute uniformly throughout the milk. Organic milk products are generally not homogenized and therefore have cream on the top.

FERMENTED DAIRY

Cultured milk products have been a part of human diet for thousands of years. Fermentation is a chemical conversion of carbohydrates into alcohols—a process that likely arose spontaneously from indigenous microflora found in milk. The pleasant taste, digestibility, and longer shelf life encouraged people to develop different fermentation methods and starter cultures. Today many of us utilize the probiotic benefits of yogurt and buttermilk to alleviate gastrointestinal distress and to stimulate the immune system. Besides being a good source of animal protein, fermented dairy contains calcium, magnesium, potassium, and vitamin B-2 and B-12.

You can easily ferment milk at home, but there are a few guidelines to remember. Keep your hands, the kitchen, and all utensils clean to discourage the growth of harmful bacteria. Use ceramic or glass containers, and avoid plastic, which allows microbes to persist. Always use fresh milk and boil it in the beginning of the fermenting process to deter any background bacteria.

Another important factor in fermentation is temperature. Various starter cultures become active in different conditions. Thermophilic lactic starter,

The Ethics of Dairy

Dedicating a chapter to dairy-based recipes shows I am not averse to using milk. However, I am aware of and saddened by animal cruelty and environmental concerns regarding dairy production today. It reveals both our greed and indifference to the suffering of others. Cows are referred to as mothers and highly esteemed in *yoga* literature. There is no excuse for mistreating them and nature. The failure to protect those dependent on us is ignorant. It highlights our lack of understanding of the spiritual kinship of all beings as eternal souls, our duty and goal of life.

The precept of nonviolence goes beyond the bodily concept of life. In the deepest sense, it means not denying oneself or someone else an opportunity for enlightenment. Offering butter, ghee, cheese, milk, and yogurt via devotional prayer and meditation has been an integral practice and a part of the yogic diet since time immemorial. It purifies the consciousness of both a yogi who makes the oblation and the cow that provides milk for it.

The power of education is stronger than boycott. Giving up dairy will not end factory farming and slaughtering. Only by cultivating knowledge about the transcendental identity, relationships, and purpose of all beings will we be able to act with an equal vision for the benefit of others.

used for making yogurt, requires a warm temperature (104–113°F/40–45°C), whereas mesophilic lactic starter, used for producing buttermilk, sour cream, and crème fraîche, does the job in a lower temperature (77–86°F/25–30°C). If the milk is hotter or cooler than these parameters indicate, the result from the starter will be unpredictable. Use a thermometer if you have one, but if you don't, estimate the temperature in comparison to your body temperature. You will quickly learn to read it

correctly by touching the milk with a finger. Once you add the starter, cover the container loosely and keep it in a draft-free environment. Also, remember to bring the starter to room temperature before adding it. When you know in which temperatures certain bacteria become active, you can use a dollop of the same yogurt as a starter and end up with two different products, yogurt and sour cream.

Humidity, which affects the rate in which the bacteria and airborne yeast grows, is perhaps the factor you can influence the least in fermenting. Therefore, compensate for the lack of control by maintaining a hygienic environment and an ideal temperature.

The easiest way to obtain a starter culture is to buy a natural yogurt or cultured buttermilk without sugar, preservatives, thickeners, or other additives, and use a tablespoon to start your batch. The package label should tell you what kind of live culture it contains.

WHEY

Whey is the liquid remaining after milk has been curdled and strained when making fresh cheese, and is a valuable ingredient in cooking. You can use it to boil vegetables, thin sauces, and bake breads. Anything cooked in whey instead of water—whether rice or vegetables—becomes richer and tastier. Because it is lightly acidic, whey prolongs cooking time and is therefore unsuitable for boiling dal and legumes. You can, however, add it to any dish at the end of cooking to enhance the flavor. Strained yogurt produces very acidic whey, which you can use to curdle milk. Store whey in a sealed container in the refrigerator for maximum two or three days.

Spices

Whole dried spices have the longest shelf life. Purchase them in bulk and store them in closed containers away from heat and light. Grind them as needed in a recipe. Their flavor is derived from volatile oils that evaporate when exposed to air. Powdering increases the contact with air and, thus, the rate of oxidation. Use a mortar and pestle to grind spices. Mustard seeds, for example, tend to become bitter when ground with an electric spice mill.

The aromatic compounds of most spices are fat soluble and become fully active when tempered in ghee or oil. Some flavoring chemicals, like vanillin in vanilla, are water soluble and will infuse food only when in contact with liquid.

The general rule is that harder to digest foods require more spicing than lighter ones. In order to create layers of flavors, most of the recipes call for adding spices in stages. Whole spices and leaves are usually fried in a small amount of ghee or oil, and powdered spices—either plain or dry-roasted—are thrown in throughout the cooking process.

Tempering is a technique in which you briefly fry whole spices and other ingredients such as grated ginger—and even fresh herbs—in a small amount of ghee or oil. It cuts the raw taste and makes the flavors bolder; in fact, it seems to wake up the latent aromatic compounds of spices and distribute them evenly in food. You may prepare tempering either at the beginning or at the end of cooking, or both.

Although the ghee or oil should be hot during tempering, I recommend moderate heat to avoid burning the spices and ruining the dish. Bigger seeds usually require a longer frying time than smaller ones. If a recipe calls for powdered spices, such as hing and black pepper, toss them in at the end of tempering. Some spices, like fenugreek, change so drastically during tempering that you have to fry them quickly. Some seeds, like black mustard, crack like popcorn, and those ingredients that contain water, like ginger and curry leaves, sputter and splatter on the pan; be careful not to burn yourself!

Olive oil is not suitable for tempering because it breaks down at high temperatures and becomes toxic. Use sunflower, rapeseed, sesame, mustard, or coconut oil instead, if you don't have ghee available. Keep in mind that oils, as a cooking medium, lend a different flavor than ghee. I have used only ghee when developing the recipes in this book and thus recommend it as a better choice.

Always consider that powdered spices change the appearance of food. Dry roasted spices, for example, darken the overall tone.

Remove whole spices, like cinnamon sticks, cardamom pods, cloves, and *tej patta* (Indian bay leaf), before serving. Seeds, like anise, *jeera* (cumin), mustard, and fennel, are small enough to be eaten as such and, in fact, offer a burst of flavor when bitten. They also add texture.

Because spices are used in such small quantities, they hardly add calories, even though many seeds contain a high ratio of fat, protein, and carbohydrates per weight. They contribute micronutrients—vitamins and minerals—essential for the body's metabolism. Many are known for their medicinal properties. Ayurveda praises spices as superfoods. They detoxify, aid digestion, calm or stimulate, and warm or cool. They affect all the senses, not just the tongue, and influence our minds, our temperaments, and our quality of life.

If you are new to spices, don't let them intimidate you. They will be demystified once you apply them in cooking. Start with tiny portions to familiarize yourself with each one's distinctive character and, then, increase the volume or complexity gradually. Spices are there to enhance palatability, not to overpower the natural features of vegetables, grains, or legumes. Because each of us has different bodily constitutions and acquired tastes, spices resonate differently with each of us. What is harmonious for one may be dull for another.

Although you may adjust the amount of salt and sugar according to your taste, don't omit them completely, because they play an important role in drawing out the full characteristics of spices.

Below is a list of the spices used throughout the book, each with a short summary and notes on the spice's curative qualities. Some of them are available in any grocery store. All of them are sold in Asian and Indian food stores around the world.

NOTE: Renunciates, pre-adolescent children, pregnant women, and the sick should avoid eating heavily spiced food, which agitates digestion and the overall constitution.

AMCHOOR

Made from sun-dried unripe mangoes, *amchoor* powder has a tart, fruity flavor. Use it in dishes where lemon-like acidity is required without added moisture. It is very mildly laxative and increases sour and astringent tastes.

ANISE

The sweetness of aniseed is similar to star anise, fennel, and licorice. It is used as a digestive aid and to relieve gas and flatulence. The seed can be ground into a powder as needed.

ASAFETIDA (HING)

Also known as *hing*, *asafetida* is resin from a perennial herb, ferula. Hing can be hard to find in a pure form outside of India. I have used in all of the recipes here Vandevi brand powdered hing, which is mixed with wheat flour as an anticaking agent. If you use another brand, you may have to experiment with the amount. Always start with a tiny pinch and increase according to your taste. Hing is a very potent spice. It is said to lower cholesterol and reduce gas.

BLACK PEPPERCORN

As an important healing spice, black peppercorn is known for its cleansing and antioxidant properties. It carries the benefits of other herbs to different parts of the body and stimulates appetite, digestion, and blood circulation. Its warming and pungent nature allows it to combine well with any other spice.

Always buy whole peppercorns and grind them as needed.

CARDAMOM (GREEN)

Cardamom has a fresh flavor, which resembles a combination of lemon zest and eucalyptus. It is considered balancing for all constitutions. Many of the recipes call for whole cardamom. Because it is quite toilsome to peel and grind when needed, you may additionally purchase powdered cardamom for baking and desserts.

CAYENNE PEPPER

Cayenne is made from red chili peppers. A natural fat burner and tonic for the heart, kidneys, lungs, pancreas, spleen, and stomach, cayenne can also raise metabolic rates by 25 percent. It contains vitamins A, B, and C. It is sold as powder.

CINNAMON (CASSIA)

Cinnamon refers to either Sri Lankan "true cinnamon" or cassia. The former is more expensive but contains only traces of the organic chemical

compound coumarin, which has shown slight toxicity to the liver and kidneys when used regularly in large amounts. The paper-thin quills are easier to grind into powder than cassia bark. The two share the same general characteristics and in terms of taste are interchangeable in most recipes. They are used in sweet and savory dishes, and enhance the bioavailability of other herbs. Cinnamon is a warming spice and contributes sweet, pungent, and bitter tastes.

For a safe use, buy organic Sri Lankan or Ceylon "true cinnamon" quills and grind them at home into powder. Unless otherwise mentioned, commercially sold cinnamon is likely cassia.

CLOVES

Cloves are the dried unopened flower buds of the evergreen clove tree and lend the pungent and astringent tastes. They combine especially well with cinnamon, coriander, jeera, and turmeric. Since it is a potent spice, use less of it instead of too much. Always buy whole cloves and grind them at home if you need clove powder.

CORIANDER

Coriander is a delicate spice that becomes stale in no time when ground, so always grind it only as needed. It's widely loved because it never masks other ingredients. It has many faces depending on how it's used. Dry roasting the seeds, for example, deepens their aroma and tone. Coriander powder is usually added toward the end of cooking for a stronger flavor.

CURRY LEAVES

These bitter leaves are potent blood purifiers. Taken regularly, they strengthen the liver and metabolism. They are a valued spleen and pancreas tonic.

Store-bought dry leaves are usually past their prime. When you find fresh leaves available in Indian stores, buy and air-dry them yourself. Tempering them briefly in ghee or oil revives their energy.

I've used small tender curry leaves in the recipes. Use a lesser amount if you purchased thicker leaves.

FENNEL

Fennel is one of the best remedies for easing digestion, both during and after the meal. It is cooling and sweet with a gentle undertone of bitterness and rich with vitamins B3 and C, potassium, magnesium, manganese, iron, and dietary fiber. It also contains flavonoids, carotenoids, camphene, and anethole. Fennel is considered stabilizing to all physical constitutions and age groups. Look for seeds that are light green and plump, instead of stale and dry.

Eating a teaspoon of fennel seeds after a meal freshens the breath and calms stomach acid.

FENUGREEK

Fenugreek is an old medicinal legume. Its leaves and seeds are edible and used as seasonings. The seeds are a bit tricky to dry roast or fry and easily become bitter. Use moderate or low temperature to avoid burning.

Fenugreek leaves, *methi*, are used fresh and dry. Potatoes seem to love them. Sprouts are easy to grow on a windowsill and add a light bitter tone to dishes (page 160).

GINGER

Fresh ginger has very different assets than the dry powder. Sometimes they are interchangeable in recipes, but mostly they are not. Drying instigates a reaction that changes the chemical makeup of ginger. As a result, dry ginger is acrid and has such a heating quality that it clears congestion by burning it away. It is especially beneficial for cold and respiratory troubles.

Fresh ginger root is analgesic, anti-inflammatory, and antibacterial. It cools the body. The juice is considered an aphrodisiac, and in most of the recipes, I urge squeezing it out before tempering. If you want, add the juice to the dish just before serving to enrich the flavor.

Choose young ginger, if possible, with a paper-thin skin. Mature ginger has a thicker skin that must be peeled off. Shred it finely to break the long fibers that add tough texture to food.

To boost your appetite and digestion, eat ½ teaspoon of finely grated, fresh ginger with a little bit of lemon juice and a pinch of salt before a meal.

GREEN CHILI

Many spices are incorrectly equated with heat. It's a misconception that discourages some to eat beyond "safe" black pepper and salt. The fact is, only chili is a *hot* spice. When consumed, the body responds—as if preparing for a traumatic event—by provoking the heart rate, increasing perspiration, and releasing endorphins that modulate appetite, release sex hormones, and highlight the feelings of euphoria.

The smaller the chilies, the hotter they are. I use Indian or Thai green chilies in my recipes. They are up to 2 inches (5 cm) long and fairly hot. I cut a small slit in them before adding them into the tempering. This method of preparation keeps the seeds intact and encapsulated by the pepper flesh so they generate less heat than if the chilies were fully split or minced. Chilies that are slit won't explode when they come in contact with hot ghee or oil. They are also easy to retrieve after cooking, before serving. When a recipe calls for chopped chilies, scrape out and discard the seeds and veins. That's where the fire is stored.

Chilies enliven the flavor, much like salt or lemon juice. They balance hard-to-digest elements, like butter, cream, ghee, or *paneer* and are, therefore, welcomed in aiding digestion in reasonable quantities. When indulged in excess, they create a fiery energy that isn't conducive for those seeking mental calm and focus.

Interestingly, chili is not native to India. None of the ancient texts, or ayurveda, speaks of it. It was introduced to India in the sixteenth century by Portuguese and Spanish explorers and quickly surpassed black pepper as the spice of choice.

JEERA (CUMIN)

Throughout the book, I refer to cumin as "jeera" to avoid confusing it with Mediterranean cumin, black cumin (*shah jeera*), kalonji (*kala jeera*), or caraway. It's a common spice and home remedy that burns impurities in the body. Taken together with coriander, it guards stomach health.

To activate jeera, dry roast or sauté it in a moderately low temperature first. If burnt, jeera becomes bitter and unappealing. Powdered jeera has a short shelf life. Always buy seeds and grind them as needed. If you are unsure what kind of cumin to buy, look for jeera in any Asian supermarket.

KALA NAMAK

Technically not a spice, *kala namak* is a mineral salt that contains sulfur. When whole, it is a brownish pink or dark violet crystal; as a powder, it has a light pinkish color. It is not fully interchangeable with salt, but it can partially replace it in some recipes. Kala namak doesn't increase the sodium level of the blood; therefore, it's a valid alternative for those with high blood pressure. It is rich in iron and known to relieve flatulence and heartburn. Kala namak is sold as both salt crystals and powder. To ensure purity, buy the former and grind it with a mortar and pestle at home.

KALONJI (NIGELLA SEEDS)

The fruits of the *Nigella sativa* plant have three to seven united follicles that carry within tiny black seeds. The seeds are used as a spice, *kalonji*. Sometimes they are wrongly called black sesame or onion seeds.

Kalonji is odorless, but when ground or chewed, it releases a faint oregano-like scent. It's a standard ingredient in Bengali cuisine and reported to be beneficial for the respiratory system. Kalonji is always sold as seeds.

LICORICE ROOT

The licorice plant is a legume, native to southern Europe and Asia. Although it isn't botanically related to anise or fennel, it's a source of similar flavoring compounds. The sweetness in licorice comes from glycyrrhizin, which is thirty to fifty times sweeter than sugar; however, its flavor is less immediate and lasts longer.

Licorice acts as an expectorant and demulcent. Traditionally, it is used to ease respiratory complaints and to soothe sore throats. It has a tendency to increase blood pressure when consumed in large quantities. In my native Scandinavia, licorice is a key component of popular salty candies. You can find dried licorice root in many health food stores. It may also go by the name black root, sweet wood, or black sugar. Added to herbal tea, it gives a naturally sweet taste.

MUSTARD SEEDS

The black mustard seeds I use in the recipes in this book are actually brownish or dark purplish and obtained from the *Brassica juncea* plant. They are different from the darker and more fiery seeds collected from *Brassica nigra* plant.

Rai (mustard seeds) are one of the oldest spices known. They are praised for their antiseptic, antibacterial, carminative, and warming properties. They are a source of omega-3 fatty acids, iron, calcium, and protein.

When black mustard seeds are dropped into hot ghee or oil, they immediately turn gray and pop and develop a nutty taste that is sharp and warming. They also can be dry roasted over moderately low heat until they crack like popcorn, then ground into a powder. In Bengali cuisine they are ground raw with poppy seeds, green chilies, and water into a paste.

NUTMEG

Nutmeg is considered a heavy spice. It has sedative qualities and dulls the mind. It's used only in low quantities, both in sweet and savory dishes. In large doses, it's reported to have psychoactive effects. Always buy it in a seed form and grate it as needed.

Drinking warm milk with a pinch of nutmeg before bedtime helps you fall asleep.

RED CHILI PEPPERS

Fresh red chili peppers are mellower than small green ones. Seeded and minced, I find them pleasant in salads.

Dry red chilies come in many sizes. They are used whole or crushed. When roasted on a dry pan, crushed chilies release fumes that cause coughing and itching in the eyes or other sensitive parts. Therefore, it is better to fry them uncrushed.

SAFFRON

Vivid crimson threads, called *stigmas*, are handpicked from *Crocus sativus* flowers, which explains why saffron is the most expensive spice worldwide.

Ayurveda recommends it for gynecological, blood, and heart-related irregularities. It's used in cooking for its unusual hay-like, honey flavor. It is sharp but sophisticated, and its uniqueness is due to the presence of the chemicals picrocrocin and safranal. It also contains crocin, which imparts a striking golden hue.

Always buy the best quality saffron with deep red threads. Powdered saffron is usually adulterated and lacks authentic flavor.

STAR ANISE

The star-shaped fruits of an evergreen tree (*Illicium verum*) native to northeast Vietnam and southwest China are harvested just before ripening. They contain *anethole*, the same effective ingredient that is in botanically unrelated aniseeds. In dishes that are simmered slowly, add star anise whole and retrieve it before serving.

TAMARIND

The tamarind tree produces fruits with several seeds contained in a hard, brown shell. The pulp is separated from the pods and seeds before it is usable for cooking. Tamarind is used as a flavoring agent when a sweet and sour taste is required.

Tamarind is acidic and sweet with faint undertones of dates. In fact, it's sometimes called the date of India. It is a source of B vitamins and calcium.

The recipes here use store-bought tamarind concentrate for practical reasons, but you can make it at home yourself. Buy peeled and pitted dry tamarind that is pressed into a small block. Break off a lime-size blob, place it in a glass or ceramic bowl, and pour a cup of boiling water over it. Cover the bowl and soak the tamarind for 15 minutes or until it softens. Finally, press it through a sieve, pushing it through with a spoon and discarding the seeds and fiber. This puree is less potent than the concentrate so adjust the recipe amount accordingly.

Tamarind is also used to polish brass and copper. Mix it with a pinch of salt and some lemon juice. Rub it with a piece of cloth onto the surface from which you want to remove tarnish and patina. Then, rinse and dry. You may have to repeat the process a few times.

TEJ PATTA

Tej patta is Indian bay leaf. It's not to be confused with bay laurel, which is cultivated in the Mediterranean and more commonly used in the United States. Tej patta belongs to the Cassia family and offers a cinnamon-like aroma, while darker green European bay leaves suggest a blend of lemon and pine. Tej patta leaves are larger with three long veins instead of a single vein and when dried have an olive green tinge. Tej patta and regular bay leaf are not interchangeable in the recipes. Even when you want to buy it in Asian store, look specifically for tej patta!

TURMERIC

Its strong yellow color signifies turmeric's role as an herb that enhances liver function. It has gotten a lot of press lately as studies have shown its potential in fighting infections, digestive disorders, and some cancers. The active proponent, *curcumin*, is a powerful antioxidant.

Turmeric has a peppery, warm, and bitter flavor. It is earthy and overpowering if used too heavily. Fresh turmeric root, which looks similar to ginger, can be finely shredded and used instead of powder. For the best quality turmeric, buy organic root or powder.

Herbs

Just about every dish tastes better with herbs. They are the leafy green parts of a plant added most often at the end of cooking for brightness. Used in small portions, like spices, they provide flavor detail rather than substance. Herbs also have culinary and medicinal value.

There's no better way to get fresh herbs than to grow them yourself, either on a windowsill or in the garden. However, fresh herbs can be found at many greenmarkets and groceries. Always buy the freshest greens you can find.

I encourage you to take advantage of the ample crop of edible wild herbs that is available in nature. Because the species of edible wild plants vary so much among tropical, dry, mild, continental, and polar climates, it's beyond the scope of this book to list them here. Please consult a botanical guide to the native vegetation of your area and find out the treasure that is waiting in the forest, savanna, or meadow. Natural weeds and flowers are bursting with *prana* (life force). Coming in closer contact with them teaches us qualities of which we can never have have too much: gratefulness, humility, and respect.

CILANTRO (FRESH CORIANDER)

Cilantro is a polarizing herb grown from coriander seeds. I've met many people who can't stand it. They usually say it tastes like gasoline or soap. Some even have an allergic reaction to it. Most people, however, respond neutrally to it and find its citrusy overtones pleasant.

Cilantro responds to heat, like most herbs, by releasing aromatic oils. Therefore, it's usually added as a garnish before serving. However, sometimes it's used in larger quantities and cooked with vegetables or pulses in order to give a mild undertone and texture to a dish.

MINT

If you've grown mint in the garden, you know it's both an aromatic and an invasive perennial. If not restricted, it will hijack the entire plot. Many cultivars and varieties of mint are available. The taxonomic Lamiaceae family includes many other cooking herbs like basil, rosemary, sage, and oregano.

Mint has a warm, refreshing flavor with a cool aftertaste. It's used in savory and sweet recipes and in chutneys and beverages.

Microgreens and Sprouts

Herbs aren't the only fresh crop we can produce at home. Microgreens are vegetable, herb, or spice seedlings used to add both visual interest and flavor. Despite their small size, they have a distinctive but not fully matured flavor. What's best, they are packed with nutrients.

It's easy to start with a pre-packaged seed mix and expand the selection as you become an expert in windowsill farming. All you need to start is a nontoxic container, organic soil, clean water, sunshine, and a bucketful of love. The seeds will germinate in a couple of days. When they develop one or two sets of leaves, it's time to harvest them by cutting the stems just above the soil line. A quick rinse and your microgreens are ready to spill the charm on the plate. Due to their high water content, cooking them is not recommended.

Microgreens are different from germinated seeds, which are known as sprouts.

Try sprouting or growing fenugreek, mustard, kale, arugula, lettuce, watercress, sunflower, beet, or radish seeds.

Rice

The reputation of basmati carrying the scent of Himalayan foothills is unfortunately tarnished today by the export of adulterated and crossbred rice that is sold as basmati around the world. The appearance, fragrance, and texture of authentic basmati are thus lost, and cooking rice, which used to be a simple act, has become unpredictable.

Raw basmati rice has a creamy white color that turns to snow-white when cooked. The length of the grain is more than thrice the breadth. Basmati is dry, unbroken, and nonsticky rice. Although nutritionally inferior to brown rice, it is easier to digest and thus suitable even for those with weak digestive energy. Because it is sattvic (pure) with a propensity to soothe and nourish bodily fluids and tissues, it is the only rice I use. It absorbs other flavors and counterbalances spices. Despite the neutral taste, it adds sweetness to the diet, which grounds and satisfies the mind. Because it builds body mass and increases mucus, I recommend those with a tendency for water retention to eat rice with moderation.

Legumes

As long as I have been a vegetarian, I have heard, ad nauseam, the argument that vegetarians do not get enough protein. It's a misconception latched to the plant-based diet like a tick. In fact, dry beans and lentils offer more than enough protein, but it's different from meat, poultry, and dairy's protein. It's considered incomplete because it lacks some of the essential amino acids found in complete protein sources. In some cases, the amino acids may be there but in inadequate proportions. However, when beans and lentils are combined with grains, such as rice, they become complete during the digestive process and offer the nutrients required for a healthy and balanced life. Offering a variety of beans, grains, nuts, and seeds in a meal is important.

Legumes are sometimes called "musical fruits" because they tend to create gas. The flatulence is caused by saponins (plant-derived chemical compounds). Saponins are also responsible for the soaplike froth that appears on the surface of the water when beans are boiling. When partially digested carbohydrates travel from the small intestine into the large one, harmless bacteria feasts on them and produces unwanted gas in the process.

To reduce the tendency for gas, soak split beans for an hour or two before cooking, and whole beans from eight hours to overnight. You may rinse and change the water a couple of times while they are soaking. Always cook beans in clean water and skim off the foam as soon as it appears. Also, use spices like chili, black pepper, ginger, jeera, mustard seeds, and hing to encourage digestion. If you are unaccustomed to eating legumes, gradually add them to your diet and give your body time to adjust to them.

Versatility is, perhaps, the best feature of legumes. They can be used whole, split, powdered, or pureed in savory and sweet dishes alike. If you want to add whey—the liquid leftover from making cheese or strained from yogurt—to soups and stews that contain pulses in order to enrich the flavor, remember that the beans must be fully cooked beforehand. Anything acidic—whey, tomatoes, tamarind, or lemon—slows down the cooking process and must be added toward the end. The same advice applies to salt and sugar. Whole spices, like cinnamon and tej patta, can be added at the beginning of cooking with turmeric and a spoonful of ghee.

Throughout the book I'm using a Sanskrit word *dal* to refer dry, split pulses or lentils. Many of the recipes are also named as dal because they present different ways of using these ingredients. Rice and dal are the power couple of my diet, around which I build the vegetable dishes, savories, salads, chutneys, and even sweets.

An endless variety of beans is available: adzuki beans, black beans, black-eyed peas, broad beans, chickpeas, kidney beans, lima beans, mung beans. . . . You name it! I've selected for the book only the ones that I use most frequently at home. Below are short descriptions of them.

CHANNA (CHICKPEAS)

The chickpea family has many members. *Channa dal* refers to split baby chickpeas, also known as *Bengali gram*. They are mainly used in dal and savory dishes and, sometimes, in sweet cakes. For a lentil, the taste is round and luscious.

Channa is slightly heavier to digest than, for example, mung, and has to be soaked and cooked longer. It makes a rich stew when slowly simmered with vegetables.

When channa is roasted and ground, it's called *besan* (chickpea flour): one of the most popular ingredients in the vegetarian world. It thickens gravies and soups, and binds koftas and patties. Chickpea flour is the main element in fritter batters, pancakes, and ghee-based sweets like *mysore pak* and *besan laddu*.

Whole chickpeas are meaty legumes. They are a source of zinc, folate, and protein. The fiber is 75 percent insoluble and remains undigested as it reaches the colon and, therefore, doesn't increase blood glucose levels; the glycemic index of chickpeas is low.

MUNG

Mung beans are small cylindrical beans with green skin and yellow insides. They are available in all supermarkets. Cooked whole, they are easy to digest, but when husked and split (referred to as *mung dal*), they become therapeutic. Yellow mung dal is the most valued food for a light, balanced diet according to ayurveda. It's the basis of *yoga* food and suitable for everyone from babies to the elderly. It detoxifies, satisfies hunger, and comforts.

Yellow mung doesn't require presoaking and cooks buttery soft in 20 minutes.

Modern nutritionists say that mung beans offer 14 grams of protein per cooked cup. They are a source of dietary fiber and phytoestrogens. They also contain vitamins A, C, and E, folate, thiamin, calcium, iron, magnesium, phosphorus, potassium, and copper.

TOOR

Toor, toovar, or *arhar* is called "pigeon bean" in English. Like channa, mung, and *urad*, it's available in Indian grocery stores. It's sold plain or coated with oil. Buy the dry kind and look for creamy golden split lentils that are shiny.

Toor dal needs to cook a little longer than mung. You can presoak it for an hour or two in warm water, drain, and roast it in a small amount of ghee over moderate heat until it turns a few shades darker before adding boiling water to it. Toor absorbs the flavors of spices well.

Sometimes figuratively called "nonvegetarian," urad is hard to digest and contains a very high amount of protein. Because it burdens the body and mind, sages and yogis abstain from it once a year, during the month of Karttika, which is devoted to enlightenment.

Urad dal looks like mung but it's black. Husked, split lentils are creamy white. Soaked and ground, they are a central ingredient in making savory pastries, fritters, and crepes. Urad and rice are fermented with fenugreek seeds for an airy and easily digested batter.

Cooked urad has a sticky consistency. The flavor is earthy.

Spelt Flour

Spelt is the new wheat, according to the U.S. Food and Drug Administration, which calls it "spelt wheat" to underline its gluten content. It isn't gluten-free or suitable for those suffering from celiac disease. However, the molecular structure of its gluten is different from wheat, which makes it more digestible. Many people who are mildly sensitive to wheat tolerate spelt.

Spelt is an ancient hybrid of Emmer wheat and *Aegilops tauschii*. During the past decade, it has resurfaced and become popular again. Thankfully so, because it's a nutritious and flavorful grain!

I haven't used wheat for years for the simple reason that spelt tastes better and has more nutrients. The husk is separated from the grain just before milling, which increases the nutritional value. Spelt is usually locally harvested and stone milled, unlike wheat, and it doesn't stay in storage for years before it reaches consumers.

Spelt is the main flour I've used and tested in the recipes here. There are several kinds of custom milled spelt flours for different needs: all-purpose, wholegrain, cake or pastry, and semolina. All-purpose spelt is moderately coarse. It's produced by removing the bran and germ of the grain, whereas wholegrain flour has both intact. Cake flour is finely ground from the innermost kernel. Spelt semolina is the gritty endosperm left behind when flour, bran, and germ are separated. Spelt is never bleached, bromated, enriched, or genetically modified.

In my recipes, spelt flour is interchangeable with wheat flour. You may have to increase the amount of liquid because wheat absorbs more moisture. Notice also that a dough or batter made with wheat flour calls for a longer kneading and mixing time because its gluten structure is different from that of spelt. You can easily overwork spelt, whereas it is hard to knead or mix wheat too much. Pay attention whether a recipe instructs you to leave the dough soft, firm, or hard, and a batter runny, moderate, or thick.

If you can't find spelt cake flour, you can substitute it with all-purpose

flour. Replace one or two tablespoons of all-purpose flour per each 1 cup (250 ml) with corn or potato starch to make the cake less dense.

Spelt has an artisanal flavor; it's nutty and robust. It contains large amounts of B complex vitamins, protein, iron, zinc, manganese, and copper.

Naturally, you get the best flour by grinding it in a small stone mill at home. It's always fresh, and you can determine the texture according to your need.

Vegetables, Fruits, and Berries

Canned and preprocessed foods have lost their luster and life force. In ayurvedic terms, they are *tamasic*, which dampens energy and promotes ignorance. Always choose fresh over canned or frozen.

Cooking with vegetables, fruits, and berries is straightforward. They require a quick rinse, peeling, and cutting. Only a few cases, presented below, require additional preparation.

COCONUT

Mature brown coconuts are available in supermarkets today. It is worth the trouble to crack open and scrape meat from a coconut at home. It takes only a few minutes longer than opening a can of coconut milk.

First rinse the coconut with water. Pierce one of the "eyes" and drain the coconut water into a bowl or glass to reserve it. Coconut water is nutritious and refreshing. Hammer the ridges of the coconut while rotating it until it splits open. Alternatively, place the coconut in a ziplock bag and whack it against a stone surface until it cracks.

Remove the coconut meat by inserting a spoon or knife between the outer shell and white meat. If you prefer pure white coconut, remove the thin, brown skin, but this step is not obligatory because the skin affects only the appearance and color.

SPINACH

Spinach stems and leaves, which are curled and wrinkled, collect soil, sand, and grit during growing and transport from the farm. Remove them by placing the spinach in a large bowl of tepid water and swishing the leaves around with your hands. Lift the leaves from the water and clean the bowl before refilling it with fresh water. You will likely find the bottom covered with dirt. Repeat the procedure until the water is clean. Drain the leaves in a colander or sieve.

Have you ever experienced a grainy mouthfeel after eating spinach? It's not due to dirt; it's caused by oxalic acid, which is sometimes excessive in spinach. Oxalic acid is water soluble, so blanching dilutes it to a degree. If you grow your own spinach organically and harvest it young, or use baby spinach, blanching is unnecessary. Whenever I buy spinach of unknown origin, I blanch it. This also sweetens the flavor, brightens the color, and softens the texture.

To blanch spinach, boil a large amount of water in a pot over high heat. Drop the washed spinach into the pot, push it under the water, and boil it for 30 seconds to 1 minute. Drain the spinach in a colander or sieve and then plunge it into a bowl of cold water to stop the cooking. Drain it again and chop it as desired.

Botanically, tomato is a fruit, but it is considered a vegetable for culinary purposes. It has been a controversial ingredient throughout history and was deemed poisonous in Britain and the North American colonies in the seventeenth century.

There is a grain of truth to its toxicity. The green parts of the plant and unripe fruits have low levels of tomatine, a toxic glycoalcaloid that has fungicidal properties. Tomatine is relatively benign to human health. However, tomatoes can have a sour effect on the gastrointestinal system even after being metabolized; they can irritate a sensitive digestive track and cause mouth and intestinal ulcers and hemorrhoids. Tomato skins are made up of cellulose, which the human body is unable to digest, and therefore, we excrete them in the same form as they were consumed. Tomatoes may exacerbate skin conditions and allergies, too. Peeling tomatoes diminishes the benefits of lycopene and beta-carotene but helps the intestines process them.

Always wash tomatoes and cut out the green stems and sockets. If you need to remove the skins from a small amount of tomatoes, use a paring knife or potato peeler. Blanch tomatoes when cooking a large quantity of them.

To blanch, boil a large amount of water in a pot over high heat. Cut a shallow cross into the skin of each tomato and drop them in the boiling water for 1 minute. Drain out the hot water and plunge the tomatoes into a bowl of cold water to stop the cooking. Drain out the water and slip off the skins with your fingers or with the help of a knife. Cut out the stem from the blanched tomatoes before using them.

Tomato seeds may be harmful to people who suffer from kidney stones and other kidney-related problems because they contain moderate amounts of oxalates, which accumulate calcium in the body. If you eat raw tomatoes, you may want to remove the seeds.

Sugar and Sweeteners

Sugar is a naturally occurring substance found in fruits, whole grains, and vegetables. A balanced diet provides us with a sufficient amount of sugar. However, eating is a social and emotional need, and we relate sweetness to comfort and pleasure. Overindulging in sugar is often a sign of stress. Everyone has experienced the adrenaline rush sugar causes. Because it turns into carbohydrates when digested, it must be burned with a physical activity. If it is allowed to accumulate in the body, it turns into fat, which contributes to weight gain, obesity, and other medical conditions.

Sugar is sugar whether it's brown, raw, or white. Use it in moderation. All sugars available, except for some syrups and honey, are processed from cane or beet juice. Needless to say, the more processed a sugar is, the less nutritional value it has.

Organic whole cane sugar has been extracted from sugar cane. White sugar has been extracted, filtered, boiled, separated, evaporated, crystallized, spun, bleached, and carbonated; and additives and synthetic chemicals have been added throughout the refinement. Between these extremes, there is a variety of "raw" sugars from dry and light brown to wet and dark.

I use both white and organic whole cane sugar in the recipes. Although I prefer the latter for its flavor and trace-mineral content, it sometimes affects the taste and appearance of food too much. White sugar is milder, sweeter, and colorless.

Honey is called *madhu*, the perfection of sweetness, in ayurvedic literature and has been a key ingredient in *amrta*, the ambrosia of gods, since time immemorial. It has a powerful therapeutic effect because of its antibacterial and antifungal properties. Honey is a healer and rejuvenator, and it increases the potency of herbs used with it. However, it should never be cooked, boiled, or baked. In high temperatures, honey becomes nonhomogenized and gluelike. As a result, it increases the toxicity of the body.

When selecting honey, look for a good quality, unprocessed honey. Unfortunately, many manufacturers mix it with sugar or syrup to lower production costs.

My personal experience is that honey is best eaten on an empty stomach. A cleansing drink made of a cup of warm water, spoonful of honey, juice of a lemon half, and pinch of black pepper is hard to beat first thing in the morning.

Salt

I have used sea salt in the recipes because it is available everywhere. It is less refined and processed than table salt, which is void of any nutritional value. In fact, the human body treats synthetically produced sodium chloride as an unnatural and toxic invader and tries to combat it by rapidly raising the blood pressure and retaining water.

Naturally occurring forms of sodium, including sea salt and Himalayan salt, are harvested and dried in the sun instead of heating them to 1200°F (650°C), which destroys alkaline minerals and trace elements that keep us hydrated, provide electrolytes, and balance the sodium-potassium ratios of the body. Less-refined salt boosts the digestive enzymes and juices that help to assimilate other vitamins and nutrients.

Ideal salt intake is relative to your health, taste, and body weight. Feel free to adjust the amount according to your preferences. Like sugar, use salt moderately and invest in quality.

Fats and Oils

The debate about fats is ongoing. As I'm writing this, finally, a war has been declared against trans fats, which are chemically produced to replace saturated fats. Once praised for the low production cost, practicality, and health benefits, trans fats have contributed to the world population becoming heavier, with an increased liability to cardiovascular disease and diabetes.

Contrary to popular belief, fats are essential to the diet. They contribute to basic body functions, hormonal balance, reproductive and skin health, and the absorption of essential vitamins. In particular, vitamins A, D, E, and K are absorbed by the body when eaten with fats. Also, essential fatty acids, including omega-3s and omega-6s, which have a role in anti-inflammatory processes, are supplied by lipids.

Ayurveda considers ghee to be the healthiest source of edible fat. It's predominated by the mode of goodness, sattva, and sacred. It's been a part of religious rituals as well as diet as long as there has been civilization. Although ghee is 50 percent saturated fat, it has short-chain fatty acids that help to strengthen and develop cell membranes. It aids digestion by stimulating the secretion of stomach acids, while other fats sit heavy in the stomach. Although milk-based, it lacks both lactose and casein, which the body is slow to process. It has antibacterial and antiviral properties promoting immunity and longevity. It lubricates and oxygenates joints and tissues. Some studies suggest that ghee lipids could lower serum cholesterol levels.

Indian communities were known to consume copious amounts of whole milk and ghee and live long, healthy lives with a nonexistent healthcare system. The epidemic of coronary disease in India begun two or three decades ago when pure ghee was replaced by adulterated mixture of fat rich in linoleic and arachidonic acids and trans fats.

The most notable effect of eating ghee is satisfaction, a characteristic of ayurvedic cooking. Mental discontent is often compensated with oversize servings that, in the long run, leave us even less satisfied rather than comforted. My observation about ghee is that it balances hunger and cravings and makes one sensitive to the feeling of fullness. Ghee helps harmonize portion sizes, and it has a destressing influence.

Ghee has a smoking point (the temperature at which oils break down and produce harmful cell-damaging oxidants) of almost 500°F (250°C), which is higher than most cooking oils—and much higher than butter! It's less likely to form dangerous radicals when it reaches high temperatures. The difference is notable when deep-frying.

When using fats in cooking, the shape of a pot plays an important role. Large, flat bottom pots require more fat because it must spread thinly over a wide area. Woks, used in the Asian kitchen, are bowl shaped for a reason. They call for less oil, the heat is evenly spread, and there is space to stir vegetables without mashing or shooting them around the kitchen. Make a tempering always in a small saucepan in order to fry the spices in the least amount of ghee or oil.

Other than ghee, I use coconut oil, extra virgin olive oil, and butter in cooking. Never heat extra virgin olive oil or butter to high temperatures.

For a healthy person, a moderate, daily dosage of fat is good. If you are suffering from high cholesterol, consult your physician regarding fat intake. Although ghee, butter, and oils are sometimes interchangeable in the recipes, they obviously have different properties that affect the taste, texture, and even color of a dish. In baking and making sweets ghee and butter yield similar results, but I would never recommend you substitute them with a margarine or shortening.

KITCHENWARE

We choose and use kitchen tools and appliances for practical purposes. However, the temperaments of delicate natural particles, found in food, and man-made machines collide sometimes. Aromas, essential oils, and other volatile compounds change their constitution—or vanish—when processed mechanically. Pressing a button instead of blending, grinding, kneading, mincing, or whipping manually might save a minute or two of physical effort, but an important element of food and the experience of being a part of a transformation, which cannot be reproduced artificially, is lost.

Labor-saving devices often increase our workload. They have tiny parts and pieces that break down, require attention and service, or clog the sink. Spare parts are rare. Once something breaks, the entire apparatus has to be replaced. Whether the kitchen gear is simple or elaborate is less crucial than keeping it clean, intact, and sharp. If you develop a habit of washing the dishes and clearing your workplace while you prepare food, you need less cookware and crockery. I find myself using the same kitchenware year after year and rarely buy additional pieces to supplement. I know exactly the abilities and potential of my pans and pots and how they nestle and brood like a flock of hens. The one whose shape and size prevent anything from boiling over is for cooking dal. Another one is for ghee: it has a thick, large bottom, like a stage on which a block of butter melts into gold. I use it for candy making as well. I also have on hand an upright saucepan for tempering spices, a French peasant pan (which is a seasoned garbon steel vessel with tall edges and natural nonstick properties) for quickly sautéing vegetables like green cabbage and kale, and of course a wok for stir-fries.

Consider the base, height, shape, volume, and material of a pot when choosing new cookware. The distribution of heat depends on these factors, which in turn impacts the cooking time, taste, texture, color, fragrance, and nutritional value of the food you are preparing.

Avoid using uncoated aluminum, lead, and scratched Teflon surfaces that may leach harmful chemicals. Anything with grooves, cracks, and rough edges tend to attract bacteria, yeast, and mold. Choose wood, stone, and metal over plastic. Wooden cutting boards, for example, can be sandpapered and oiled repeatedly in order to keep them hygienic and functional.

The recipes in this book don't call for special cooking accessories or utensils. There are, however, a few useful items that I'd like to point out.

Cheesecloth is one of them. If you are new to making fresh cheese or strained yogurt at home, you may want to purchase a pair of 100 percent cotton weave, double layer cloth diapers or a piece of muslin (gauze) cotton.

A quick-release ice cream scoop is a creative and versatile tool for making drop cookies, frying *vadas* and *pakoras,* and scraping out pumpkin seeds.

A large stone mortar and pestle is a necessity for grinding dry and wet ingredients.

A perforated or slotted spoon is designed to quickly drain fats while stirring, turning, and retrieving fried items.

A loaf pan, springform cake pan, muffin tin, pie pan or plate, and tart pans are some of the bakeware you may want to have on hand before diving into the dessert section of the book.

A thermometer, kitchen scale, measuring cups, and measuring spoons are reassuring, especially if you are an inexperienced cook.

My top recommendations for special kitchen accessories are vinyl gloves and a first aid kit. The former is priceless when peeling and cutting beets, chilies, and ginger, and the latter comes in handy when a knife inevitably slips.

FOOD PREPARATION: Bowls, citrus reamer, cutting boards, grater, ice cream scoop, ladle, large liquid measuring cup, measuring spoons, mortar and pestle, paring knife, peeler, slotted spoon, spatulas, spoons, strainer, tongs, turner, vegetable knife, whisk, wooden utensils

COOKING: Frying pan, cast-iron pans, grill or griddle pan, stainless steel pots, ovenproof dishes, ramekins, small saucepan, wok or a stir-fry pan

BAKEWARE: Baking sheets or oven trays, cookie cutters, cooling racks, cupcake liners, flour sifter, loaf pan, muffin tins, pastry brush, pastry wheel, piping bag and tips, rolling pin, rubber spatula, springform cake pan, tart pans

APPLIANCES: Blender, electric spice mill, food processor, hand mixer, immersion blender

ACCESSORIES: Apron, rolls of parchment paper and plastic wrap, cheesecloth, cleaning materials, knife sharpener, oven mitt, a trivet, scale, tea towels, timer, vinyl gloves, first aid kit

STORAGE AND ORGANIZING: Various sizes of lidded containers, glass jars, spice jars

SERVING: Bowls, cutlery, dinnerware, glassware, ladles, pitchers, platters, spoons

Conversion Table

{TEASPOON}

⅛ tsp = 0.63 ml = a pinch
¼ tsp = 1.25 ml
½ tsp = 2.5 ml
¾ tsp = 3.75 ml
1 tsp = 5 ml
2 tsp = 10 ml
3 tsp = 1 Tbsp

{TABLESPOON}

1 Tbsp = 15 ml
2 Tbsp = 30 ml
3 Tbsp = 45 ml
4 Tbsp = 60 ml
4 Tbsp + ½ tsp = 63 ml = ¼ cup
5 Tbsp = 75 ml
5 Tbsp + 1½ tsp = 83 ml = ⅓ cup

{MILLILITER/CUP}

½ cup = 125 ml
⅔ cup = 167 ml (150 ml + 1 Tbsp + ½ tsp)
¾ cup = 188 ml (175 ml + 2½ tsp)
1 cup = 250 ml
2 cups = 500 ml
3 cups = 750 ml
4 cups = 1000 ml = 1 liter
8 cups = 2000 ml = 2 liters

{TEMPERATURE}

100°F = 38°C
125°F = 52°C
200°F = 100°C
300°F = 150°C
350°F = 180°C
400°F = 200°C
425°F = 220°C

{LENGTH}

1 inch = 2.5 cm
2 inch = 5 cm
3 inch = 7.5 cm

{FINE SEA SALT}

1 tsp fine sea salt = 6 g
1 Tbsp fine sea salt = 18 g

{REFINED (WHITE) SUGAR}

1 tsp refined sugar = 5 g
1 Tbsp refined sugar = 15 g
1 cup (250 ml) refined sugar = 228 g

{ORGANIC WHOLE CANE SUGAR}

1 tsp whole cane sugar = 3 g
1 Tbsp whole cane sugar = 9 g
1 cup (250 ml) whole cane sugar = 180 g

{ALL-PURPOSE SPELT FLOUR}

1 cup (250 ml) all-purpose spelt flour = 120 g

{SPELT CAKE FLOUR}

1 cup (250 ml) spelt cake flour = 120 g

{WHOLEGRAIN SPELT FLOUR}

1 cup (250 ml) wholegrain spelt flour = 140 g

{SPLIT CHANNA, MUNG, TOOR,
AND URAD DAL}

1 cup (250 ml) dal = 220 g

{BASMATI RICE}

1 cup (250 ml) basmati rice = 225 g

{IDLI RICE}

1 cup (250 ml) idli rice = 230 g

{GHEE}

1 Tbsp ghee = 15 g

{OIL}

1 Tbsp oil = 13 g

GLOSSARY

Ahimsa: Nonviolence means not to injure the body, mind, or soul. It arises from the premise that all living beings are equal sparks of divine energy. Those who have a more developed mental and intellectual faculty and less covered consciousness should look after and uplift the simpler forms of life, instead of exploiting and abusing them for selfish purposes. Although a vegetarian diet generally involves less cruelty than one that includes meat, it is still considered impure as long as it doesn't address the spiritual needs of those involved in the food chain. Yoga cuisine is founded on the practice of connecting all energies to the energetic, and the soul to the Supreme through meditation and prayer.

Akasha: Ethereal space, one of the five physical elements and the basis of all things material. Its characteristic is sound, and it expands into air, fire, water, and earth and their corresponding senses and sense objects. In addition to these elements, there are three subtle cosmic principles—mind, intelligence, and false ego—that form the astral body and are constantly pulled by the tendencies of goodness (*sattva*), passion (*rajas*), and ignorance (*tamas*), which are like invisible strings that over time entangle living beings into the intricacies of action (*karma*) and the cycle of birth and death (*samsara*). The Vedic literature compares the material world to an upside-down reflection of the spiritual reality. Understanding the illusory nature of the mirror image is called moksha, or liberation, and is a preliminary stage of spiritual life.

Asana: Both the place and posture in which a yoga practitioner sits. Sukhasana (easy pose) simply means sitting cross-legged. *Sukha* refers to happiness, joyfulness, and comfort. This asana promotes a physical and mental balance in order to draw the attention inward. Padmasana (lotus posture) requires more flexibility because the feet are placed on top of the opposing thighs. In traditional Indian homes, meals are taken with all guests seated in asana on the floor.

Ashrama: Either a physical place or a state of mind in which spiritual culture is continually practiced; the more familiar form of the word is ashram.

Ayurveda: An ancient practice of medicine that translates as "life knowledge." It emphasizes building a vital metabolic system, strong digestion, and proper excretion by offering dietary recommendations that balance bodily and mental equilibrium. As a holistic approach to nutrition and health, it examines the potency of food also in terms of where, when, with whom, and in what kind of ambience it is produced, served, and consumed. All the recipes in this book follow sattvic guidelines when eaten in moderation and present the six tastes by which ayurveda describes all foods: sweet, sour, salty, pungent, bitter, and astringent. Different combinations of these tastes affect the primordial elements—earth, water, fire, air, and akasha—within the body.

Ayurveda recognizes three basic body constitutions—*vata* (*akash* and air), *pitta* (fire and to a lesser degree water), and *kapha* (earth and water)—called *dosha*, of which one is usually more prominent than the others, but it is not uncommon that a person's physique is a mixture of two or all three types. Disturbances appear when foods aggravate the elements. When you understand your body type, you can increase your well-being by adapting a supporting and stabilizing diet.

Earth and water elements dominate the sweet taste, earth and fire elements dominate the sour taste, water and fire elements dominate the salty taste, air and fire elements dominate the pungent taste, air and akasha dominate the bitter taste, and air and earth elements dominate the astringent taste.

Sweet foods include sugar, rice, milk, cream, butter, ghee, and wheat products. Sour foods include lemons, cheese, yogurt, tomatoes, grapes, oranges, berries, and other sour fruits. Salty foods are self-explanatory and include salt and sea vegetables. Pungent foods include cayenne, chili peppers, radishes, ginger, and horseradish. Bitter foods include bitter melon, endive, chicory, mustard greens, parsley, sprouts, kale, spinach, chard, brussels sprouts, zucchini, celery, sprouts, beets, and grapefruit. Astringent foods include beans, lentils, dal, pomegranates, apples, pears, broccoli, asparagus, green beans, rye, buckwheat, quinoa, hing, and turmeric.

Different combinations of tastes balance different *doshas*. For instance, increased amounts of sweet, sour, and salty tastes balance *vata*; increased amounts of sweet, bitter, and astringent tastes balance *pitta*; and increased amounts of pungent, bitter, and astringent tastes balance *kapha*.

Bhakti-Yoga: Bhakti means uninterrupted, favorable service to Krishna or God; bhakti-yoga is the method of reviving one's constitutional position and acting for the purpose of developing transcendental love.

Jagannatha Mandir: In the Odhisan town of Puri, there is a sacred temple dedicated to Jagannatha, the Lord of the universe. The English word *juggernaut* originates from the annual festival of bringing the brightly painted wooden deities of Jagannatha, Subhadra, and Balarama in chariots decorated with giant colorful canopies to the street, where everyone can worship them. Royalty and dignitaries dress as sweepers and sweep the street in front of the wagons. This important *vaishnava* (related to Vishnu) celebration that saints, poets, and scriptures glorify as a highly auspicious event is one of the major pilgrimage destinations for millions of people. Srila Abhay Charan Bhaktivedanta Swami Prabhupada brought this Ratha-yatra procession to New York, London, and other major Western cities in the 1960s.

Mahatma: A great soul.

Mudra: A sophisticated hand position. In elaborate Vedic temple practice, or *pooja*, mudras have been used since time immemorial. The tradition resembles sign language, but it is intended to purify and fix the worshipper's mind to a ritual's inner substance and bring joy to the object of worship.

Prasadam (and Mahaprasadam): Items offered to the Supreme with a loving intention and then honored as sacred gifts. *Mahaprasadam* means great mercy and refers to the remnants of an exalted person or divinity that no longer entangle materially but purify and elevate spiritually. The process of sanctifying food has a rich history in Vedic literature and stands for a selfless devotion in the bhakti tradition. Giving up the mentality of "I and mine" by sacrificing the need to control and enjoy is an elementary discipline in all authentic yoga lineages.

Sattva: The material qualities of nature—goodness (*sattva*), passion (*rajas*), and ignorance (*tamas*)—enable our mental, emotional, and physical experiences of the universe. Through these modes, the created nature manifests the manner of behavior that directs our value judgment and actions. Goodness, passion, and ignorance are the measures of interaction between a conscious spirit soul and unconscious matter, and may be compared to the primary colors, yellow, red, and blue. The consciousness, which may be compared to clear light, becomes conditioned under the influence of the modes, just like a beam of light becomes colored when passing through a prism.

Of the three, sattva is pure and illuminating. It increases happiness and knowledge, whereas rajas, which is characterized by longings and desires, is impossible to satiate. Tamas binds the soul to darkness, indolence, and sleep.

Anyone who aspires to improve the quality of life has to associate with knowledge, situations, persons, actions, and goals that promote sattva.

Sri Krishna: *Krishna* is a Sanskrit word for "all attractive" and suggests that all qualities we perceive and value expand from a divine origin. Vaishnava followers of the Vedas or bhakti practitioners approach Sri Krishna as *bhagavan:* the source of all incarnation, the possessor of all energies, and the personification of all *rasa* or loving mellows arising from relationships. This is an intimate conclusion of reality, based on dynamic and fulfilling interaction between the Supreme Person and unlimited energies, of which every *jiva* or individual soul is a part of.

Taittiriya Upanishad: The Upanishads are a collection of 108 philosophical dissertations. The word *upa-ni-sat* means to sit closely and refers to a disciple sitting close to his teacher in order to receive transcendental wisdom. By establishing the nonmaterial quality of the Absolute, the Upanishads prepare the way for understanding the transcendental personality, *bhagavan*, who possesses all spiritual opulence and is the ultimate object of meditation and devotion.

Taittiriya Upanishad describes the various degrees of happiness enjoyed by the different beings in creation.

Vedic Culture: The practical application of philosophy contained in the Vedas.

Vedic Literature: Although ancient, Vedic literature is neither dead nor archaic. The word *Veda* comes from the Sanskrit root *vid*, which means to know and refers to knowledge that was transmitted orally by the sages of India until, about five thousand years ago, Srila Vyasadeva compiled it in a literary form. The original scriptures—Rig Veda, Yajur Veda, Sama Veda, Atharva Veda—as well as Upanishads, Puranas, Vedanta-sutra, Mahabharata, Bhagavad-gita, and so forth are meant for the elevation of mankind by educating about the nature, interaction, and goal of a living being (*jiva*) in his relation to the Absolute (*ishvara*), material nature (*prakrti*), time factor (*kala*), and activities (*karma*).

RESOURCES

Organic Indian Groceries and Spices Online

IN USA:

Indian Foods Co.: store.indianfoodsco.com
iShopIndian: www.ishopindian.com
Pure Indian Foods: www.pureindianfoods.com

IN CANADA:

Gathering Place Trading Company: www.gatheringplacetrading.com
Spice Sanctuary: www.spicesanctuary.com
The Spice Trader: www.thespicetrader.ca

IN EUROPE:

Pinch Seasonings: www.pinchseasonings.co.uk
Seasoned Pioneers: www.seasonedpioneers.co.uk
Steenbergs Organic: www.steenbergs.co.uk

IN AUSTRALIA:

Nature Shop: www.natureshop.com.au
Pure Food Essentials: www.purefoodessentials.com
Santos Organics: santostrading.com.au

Books by My Cooking Gurus

KURMA DASA (HTTP://KURMA.NET):

Cooking with Kurma (Bhaktivedanta Book Trust, 1998)
Great Vegetarian Dishes (Mandala, 1990)
Quick Vegetarian Dishes: Recipes You Can Prepare in a Hurry (Mandala, 2001)
Vegetarian World Food (Mandala, 2005)

YAMUNA DEVI:

Lord Krishna's Cuisine: The Art of Indian Vegetarian Cooking (Dutton, 1978)
Yamuna's Table: Healthful Vegetarian Cuisine Inspired by the Flavors of India (Dutton, 1992)

Pure Vegetarian Restaurants Worldwide
www.iskconcenters.com/restaurants

About Bhakti-Yoga
www.krishna.com

My Charitable Causes
Bhaktivedanta Academy: www.bhaktivedantaacademy.com
Care for Cows: www.careforcows.org
Food for Life: www.ffl.org
Healthcare: www.bhaktivedantahospital.com

INDEX

A

ahimsa (nonviolence), 2, 291
almonds
    Almond Halva, 207
    Laddu (Chickpea Confection
      with Orange Zest), 227
Aloo Bonda (potato balls), 149
aluminum pots, 287
amchoor, 263
Amrakhand (Sweet Mango Yogurt),
    211
anethole, in anise, 269
animal cruelty, 258
anise, star, 263, 270
Apple Chutney, 188
apples
    Apple Chutney, 188
    Warm Apple Cider, 251
appliances, basic needs, 288
arhar. See toor ("pigeon bean")
artichokes
    Braised Artichoke Salad, 175
    preparing, 175
asafetida (hing), 263
asana (poses, posture), 291
ashram (place of self-realization),
    9, 291
atithidevo bhava (gift-giving), 16
avocados
    Avocado Paratha (Avocado
      Flatbread), 145
    Red Cabbage, Beets, and Avo-
      cado Salad, 172
ayurveda
    approach to healing, 291–92
    dosha (basic body constitutions),
      292
    and drinking water at meals, 19
    ghee, 284
    healing properties of takra, 38
    properties of milk, 250
    recommendations for eating and
      drinking, 19

role of ghee, 284
saffron, 268
and spices as superfoods, 262
tamasic foods, 280
yellow mung dal, 277

B

Baby Potatoes in Yogurt-Tomato
    Sauce, 115
bakeware, basic needs, 288
bananas
    Banana and Berry Ice Cream,
      219
    Banana Raita, 196
Basic Dal, 64
Basmati Rice, 67
bay leaf, Indian, 271
beets
    Beet and Carrot Juice, 246
    Beet Kofta in Sour Cream
      Sauce, 99–100
    Red Cabbage, Beets, and Avo-
      cado Salad, 172
Bengali cuisine
    Bengali-Style Vegetables with
      Ground Mustard Seed, 126–27
    Bhapa Doi (Steamed Yogurt
      Custard), 200–201
    customs around meals, 18
    kalonji (nigella seeds) in, 267
    mustard seeds in, 268
    Panch Phoron (spice mix), 57
    radhuni in, 57
    Saffron Sandesh, 241
    Singara, 150–53
Bengali gram (channa / chickpeas), 277
berries, fresh
    Banana and Berry Ice Cream,
      219
    Berry Soup, 224
Berry Soup, 224
beverages
    Beet and Carrot Juice, 246

Golden Milk, 250
Lime and Cucumber Drink, 244
Pomegranate Juice, 245
Savory Green Smoothie, 247
Savory Lassi, 249
Strawberry Lassi, 248
Takra (Churned Yogurt Drink), 38
Warm Apple Cider, 251
Yogi Tea, 252
bhakti-yoga, 9, 231, 292
Bhapa Doi (Steamed Yogurt
    Custard), 200–201
bitter melon (karela)
    Bitter Melon Crisps, 92
    as an ingredient, 92
blanching
    spinach, 280
    tomatoes, 282
Braised Artichoke Salad, 175
Broth, Savory Buttermilk, 41
Brussels Sprouts in Savory Cream,
    96
Butter, homemade, 22
buttermilk
    buttermilk broth, 38
    cultured, homemade, 30
    Savory Buttermilk Broth, 41

C

cabbage
    Cabbage and Kale with Ground
      Poppy Seeds, 91
    Cabbage Kofta, 103–4
    Kale and Cabbage Chips, 156
    Red Cabbage, Beets, and
      Avocado Salad, 172
cacao powder, as an ingredient, 231
cake flour, 278–79
cakes
    Cherry and Chocolate Layer
      Cake, 232–35
    Lemon and Coconut Sponge
      Cakes, 215

candy. *See* confections, candies
canned foods, 280
caramel
  Caramel Fudge, 204
  caramel sauce, 232–35
  Lemon and Caramel Tartlets,
    222–23
cardamom (green), 263
carob powder, as an ingredient, 231
carrots
  Beet and Carrot Juice, 246
  Carrot and Pumpkin Soup, 124
  Kheer (Carrot Pudding), 237
cashew nuts
  Cashew Chutney, 180
  Chickpea Rice Salad with Ca-
    shews and Microgreens, 163
  Lemon Rice with Cashews, 71
cassia (cinnamon), 263–65
Cauliflower Coconut Curry with
  Peas and Fresh Cheese, 108
celeriac, in Root Vegetable Frites,
  107
Chaat Masala (spice mix), 61
channa (chickpeas). *See* chickpeas
cheese, fresh (*chenna*). *See also*
  yogurt cheese
  Cauliflower Coconut Curry with
    Peas and Fresh Cheese, 108
  Chenna / Paneer (Fresh Pressed
    Cheese), 42–43
  Chenna Poda (Sweet Cheese
    Pastry), 220
  Fried Cheese Balls, 45
  Fried Cheese Cubes, 46
  Kalakand (Sweet Cheese Con-
    fection), 212
  Palak Paneer (Spinach and Fresh
    Cheese), 112
  Saffron Sandesh, 241
  Yogurt Cheese, 37
Cheese Balls, Fried, Green Bean
  Tomato Curry with, 111
cheesecake, Chenna Poda (Sweet
  Cheese Pastry), 220
cheesecloth, 287
chenna. See cheese, fresh (*chenna*)
Cherry and Chocolate Layer Cake,
  232–35

cherry sauce, 232–35
chickpeas (*channa*), chickpea flour
  channa dal, 75, 277
  Chickpea Confection with Or-
    ange Zest (Laddu), 227
  Chickpea Rice Salad with Ca-
    shews and Microgreens, 163
  as an ingredient, 277
  Khandvi, 146–47
  Laddu (Chickpea Confection
    with Orange Zest), 227
chili, green
  as an ingredient, 266–67
  Khandvi, 146–47
chili peppers, red, 268
chocolate, cocoa
  Cherry and Chocolate Layer
    Cake, 232–35
  as an ingredient, 231
  and yoga cuisine, 231
chutney
  Apple Chutney, 188
  Cashew Chutney, 180
  Coconut Chutney, 181
  Date and Tamarind Chutney, 183
  Gooseberry Chutney, 184
  Plum Chutney, 187
  Tomato Chutney, 191
cilantro (fresh coriander)
  as an ingredient, 273
  Peas with Paneer and Cilantro,
    119
cinnamon (cassia)
  as an ingredient, 263–65
  in garam masala, 58
  in sambar powder, 54
cleanliness, 16–17
cloves, 265
coconut
  Cauliflower Coconut Curry
    with Peas and Fresh Cheese,
    108
  Coconut Chutney, 181
  Coconut Rice with Saffron, 68
  as an ingredient, 280
  Lemon and Coconut Sponge
    Cakes, 215
confections, candies
  Almond Halva, 207

Caramel Fudge, 204
Fruit and Nut Energy Bars, 228
Gopinath (Cacao Hazelnut
  Fudge), 231
Kalakand (Sweet Cheese
  Confection), 212
Laddu (Chickpea Confection
  with Orange Zest), 227
Melt-in-the-Mouth Candy, 216
Pecan and Hazelnut Fudge, 203
Saffron Sandesh, 241
Strawberry Halva, 208
conversion table, basic measurements, 289
cooking
  conscious, 1–2
  and fulfillment, 9–10
  and hospitality, 16
  pure vegetarian, 10–11
coriander
  dried, 265
  fresh (cilantro), 273
Crème Fraîche, 33
crepes
  Rice and Dal Crepes, 139–40
  Semolina Crepes, 136
crust, for pies, 238
cucumbers
  Lime and Cucumber Drink, 244
  Summer Salad with Edible
    Flowers, 167
Cultured Buttermilk, 30
cumin (*jeera*), black cumin (*shah
  jeera*), 267
curcumin, 271
curries
  Cauliflower Coconut Curry
    with Peas and Fresh Cheese,
    108
  Green Bean Tomato Curry with
    Fried Cheese Balls, 111
  Potato Curry from Mathura, 116
  Pumpkin and Spinach Curry, 123
Curry Leaf Powder (Ground Sweet
  Neem), 50
curry leaves
  Eggplant Lentil Sambar with
    Curry Leaves, 83
  as an ingredient, 265

Curry Powder variations, 53
custards, Bhapa Doi, 200–201
cutting boards, 287

D

dairy
    ethics of, 258
    fermented, 257–59
    milk, organic whole, 257
    whey, 259
dal (split pulses or lentils)
    Basic Dal, 64
    building diet around, 15, 275
    channa dal, 75
    Eggplant Lentil Sambar with
        Curry Leaves, 83
    Green Mango Dal, 76
    Green Mung Dal with Fennel,
        72
    Jagannath Dal, 75
    Kitchari (Rice and Dal Por-
        ridge), 79
    mung dal, 277
    Rice and Dal Crepes, 139–40
    toor dal, 277
    urad dal, 278
Date and Tamarind Chutney, 183
dinner, light, benefits of, 18
Donne, John, 8–9
dosas (rice and lentil crepes), aloo
    bonda filling for, 149
dosha (basic body constitutions),
    292
dough
    Avocado Paratha, 145
    pie crust, 238
    Poori, 130
    Roti, 133
    Singara, 150
Doughnuts, Lentil (Vada), 142
dressing
    Chickpea Rice Salad with Ca-
        shews and Microgreens, 163
    Red Cabbage, Beets, and Avo-
        cado Salad, 172
    Sour Cream Dressing, 29
    Summer Salad with Edible
        Flowers, 167
drinking during meals, 18–19

E

eating
    with fingers, benefits of, 18
    place settings, 17
    seating, 17
    serving guests first, 18
    and yogic etiquette, 17
eggplant
    Eggplant Lentil Sambar with
        Curry Leaves, 83
    Eggplant Raita, 197
    Quick Eggplant Pickle, 195
essential fatty acids, 284

F

fasting, 10
fats and oils, importance in diet,
    284. *See also* ghee
fennel/fennel seeds
    Green Mung Dal with Fennel, 72
    as an ingredient, 265
fenugreek (*methi*)
    Fenugreek Leaves, 160
    as an ingredient, 266
fermented dairy products, 257–59
fingers, eating with, 18
Finland, school mealtimes, 5
flatbread. *See* paratha (flatbread)
flatulence, from legumes, 275
flour, for cake, 232–35, 278–79
flour, spelt, benefits over wheat
    flour, 278
flowers, edible, in Summer Salad,
    167
food
    canned, preprocessed, 280
    and conscious cooking, 1–2
    and fulfillment, 9–10
    and hospitality, 16
    making educated choices about,
        10–11
    and relationships, 1
    serving, 18
    touching food when eating, 18
Fried Cheese Balls, 45
Fried Cheese Cubes, 46
fritters (Yogurt Cheese Pakora), 155
Fruit and Nut Energy Bars, 228
fudge

Caramel Fudge, 204
Gopinath (Cacao Hazelnut
    Fudge), 231
Melt-in-the-Mouth Candy, 216
Pecan and Hazelnut Fudge, 203

G

Garam Masala (spice mix), 58
garlic, avoiding, 10
ghee
    cooking with, 284
    Ghee (basic recipe), 25
    satisfaction from eating, 284
    seasoned, 25
    as source of fat, 284
    using for tempering, 260
gift-giving, and hospitality, 16
ginger
    grated, as meal accompaniment,
        17
    as an ingredient, 266
    Khandvi (chili-ginger flavored
        snack), 146–47
Golden Milk, 250
Gooseberry Chutney, 184
Gopinath (Cacao Hazelnut Fudge),
    231
green beans
    Green Bean Tomato Curry with
        Fried Cheese Balls, 111
    Spiced Green Beans, 88
green chili, 266–67
Green Mango Dal, 76
Green Mung Dal with Fennel, 72
greens, mixed
    Savory Green Smoothie, 247
    Wilted Green Salad, 171
Ground Sweet Neem (Curry Leaf
    Powder), 50
Gujarati cuisine
    Amrakhand (Sweet Mango
        Yogurt), 211
    Khandvi (chili-ginger flavored
        snack), 146–47

H

halvas
    Almond Halva, 207
    Strawberry Halva, 208

hazelnuts
  Gopinath (Cacao Hazelnut Fudge), 231
  Pecan and Hazelnut Fudge, 203
herbs
  cilantro (fresh coriander), 273
  fresh, wild, as an ingredient, 273
  Herb Salad with Pea Shoots and Pistachio, 164
  mint leaves, 273
Himalayan salt, 283
hing (asafetida), 263
homogenization, 257
honey (madhu), 283
hospitality, 16

I

Ice Cream, Banana and Berry, 219
ice cream scoop, 288
ingredients
  dairy, 257–59
  fats and oils, 284–85
  flours, 278
  herbs, 273
  honoring when using, 10
  legumes/beans, 275–78
  microgreens and sprouts, 273–74
  rice, 274
  salt, 283
  spices, 260–71
  sugars and sweeteners, 282–83
  vegetables, fruits, and berries, 280–82

J

Jagannath Dal, 75
Jagannath, Sri
  channa dal offering for, 75
  Chenna Poda, 220
  festival in Puri, 75, 292–93
Jagannatha Mandir, 292–93
jeera (cumin), 267

K

Kalakand (Sweet Cheese Confection), 212
kala namak, 267
kale

Cabbage and Kale with Ground Poppy Seeds, 91
Kale and Cabbage Chips, 156
kalonji (nigella seeds), 267
karela. See bitter melon
karma (actions and reactions), 10
Karnataka region, Melt-in-the-Mouth Candy, 216
Khandvi (chili-ginger flavored snack), 146–47
Kheer (Carrot Pudding), 237
kitcharis (khichdi, kitchuri)
  Kitchari (Rice and Dal Porridge), 79
  Quinoa Kitchari, 80
kitchen measurements, conversion table, 289
kitchenware
  accessories, 288
  aluminum pots, 287
  appliances, 288
  bakeware, 288
  basic considerations, 287
  cheesecloth, 287
  cutting boards, 287
  ice cream scoop, 288
  mortar and pestle, stone, 288
  pots, new, choosing, 287
  serving equipment, 288
  slotted spoon, 288
  spoon, slotted, 288
  storage containers, 288
koftas (dumplings)
  Beet Kofta in Sour Cream Sauce, 99–100
  Cabbage Kofta, 103–4
Krishna, Sri, 293–94

L

Laddu (Chickpea Confection with Orange Zest), 227
lassis
  Savory Lassi, 249
  Strawberry Lassi, 248
legumes/beans
  benefits of, 275
  channa (chickpeas), 277
  varieties/versatility, 275
lemon

Lemon and Caramel Tartlets, 222–23
Lemon and Coconut Sponge Cakes, 215
Lemon Rice with Cashews, 71
  as meal accompaniment, 17
lentils. See also dal (split pulses or lentils)
  Eggplant Lentil Sambar with Curry Leaves, 83
  Vada (Lentil Doughnuts), 142
licorice root, 267–68
Lime and Cucumber Drink, 244
love, expressing through food, 10

M

madhu (honey), 283
mahaprasadam, 293
mahaprashad (great mercy), 75
Maharashtrian cuisine, Amrakhand (Sweet Mango Yogurt), 211
mahatma, meaning, 293
mango
  Amrakhand (Sweet Mango Yogurt), 211
  Green Mango Dal, 76
Mathura, Potato Curry from, 116
meals, composing, 18–19
mealtimes
  formal, during author's childhood, 2–5
  at school, conviviality of, 5
  yoga etiquette, 5
Melt-in-the-Mouth Candy, 216
methi (fenugreek leaves), 266
microgreens and sprouts
  Chickpea Rice Salad with Cashews and Microgreens, 163
  as an ingredient, 273–74
milk
  Golden Milk, 250
  healthful properties, 250
  organic whole, 257
mint leaves
  as an ingredient, 273
  Watermelon Salad with Toasted Sunflower Seeds, 168
mortar and pestle, stone, 288
mudra (hand position), 293

mung beans, 277
mung dal, 277
mushrooms, avoiding, 10
mustard seeds
    Bengali-Style Vegetables with
      Ground Mustard Seed, 126–27
    as an ingredient, 268
    as substitute for *radhuni*, 57

N

Neem, Ground Sweet (Curry Leaf
    Powder), 50
nigella seeds (*kalonji*), 267
nonviolence (*ahimsa*), and cooking,
    2
North Indian cuisine
    Garam Masala, 58
    Palak Paneer (Spinach and Fresh
      Cheese), 112
nutmeg, 268
nuts, mixed
    Fruit and Nut Energy Bars, 228
    Savory Green Smoothie, 247

O

Odisha cuisine
    Chenna Poda (Sweet Cheese
      Pastry), 220
    Jagannath Dal, 75
    radhuni in, 57
oils for tempering, 260
Okra, Spiced, 95
olive oil, 260
onions, avoiding, 10
Orange Zest, Chickpea Confection
    with Orange Zest (Laddu), 227
Oriya cuisine, 18
out-of-body experience, 6–8

P

Pakora, Yogurt Cheese, 155
Panch Phoron (spice mix), 57
paneer
    Chenna / Paneer (Fresh Pressed
      Cheese), 42
    Fried Cheese Cubes, 46
    making paneer, 43
    Palak Paneer (Spinach and Fresh
      Cheese), 112

Peas with Paneer and Cilantro, 119
pressing, 42
paratha (flatbread), avocado, 145
pasteurization, 257
Peach Pie with Heart-Shaped Crust,
    238
peas
    Cauliflower Coconut Curry
      with Peas and Fresh Cheese,
      108
    Herb Salad with Pea Shoots and
      Pistachio, 164
    Peas with Paneer and Cilantro,
      119
Pecan and Hazelnut Fudge, 203
peppercorn, black, 263
pickles, eggplant, 195
pies
    Peach Pie with Heart-Shaped
      Crust, 238
    savory (singara), 150–53
"pigeon bean" (*toor*). *See* toor ("pi-
    geon bean")
Pistachio Nuts, Herb Salad with Pea
    Shoots and, 164
Plum Chutney, 187
Pomegranate Juice, 245
Poori, 130
Poppy Seeds, Ground, Cabbage and
    Kale with, 91
porridges
    Kitchari (Rice and Dal Por-
      ridge), 79
    Quinoa Kitchari, 80
    Upma, 84
posture, when eating, 17
potatoes
    Aloo Bonda (potato balls), 149
    Baby Potatoes in Yogurt-Tomato
      Sauce, 115
    Potato Curry from Mathura, 116
pots
    choosing, 287
    shape of, and fat use, 284
    for tempering, 285
prana (life force), in living plants, 273
prasadam (grace), 10, 293
preprocessed foods, 280
Pudding, Carrot (Kheer), 237

pumpkin
    Carrot and Pumpkin Soup, 124
    Pumpkin and Spinach Curry, 123
pure vegetarian, defined, 10–11
Puri, Odisha, temple dedicated to
    Jagannatha, 75, 292–93
purification, 16–17

Q

Quick Eggplant Pickle, 195
Quinoa Kitchari, 80

R

rai (mustard seeds), 268
raitas
    Banana Raita, 196
    Eggplant Raita, 197
rajas (passion), 293
raspberries, in Berry Soup, 224
raw sugar, 283
Red Cabbage, Beets, and Avocado
    Salad, 172
red chili peppers, 268
rice
    Basmati Rice, 67
    building diet around, 275
    Chickpea Rice Salad with Ca-
      shews and Microgreens, 163
    Coconut Rice with Saffron, 68
    as an ingredient, 274
    Kitchari (Rice and Dal Por-
      ridge), 79
    Lemon Rice with Cashews, 71
    as meal accompaniment, 15
    Rice and Dal Crepes, 139–40, 149
roasted vegetables
    basic recipe, 120
    Bengali-Style Vegetables with
      Ground Mustard Seed, 126–27
Root Vegetable Frites, 107
Roti, 133–35

S

saffron
    Coconut Rice with Saffron, 68
    as an ingredient, 268–70
    Tomato Sauce with Saffron, 192
Saffron Sandesh, 241
salt, 283

sambar
    Eggplant Lentil Sambar with
      Curry Leaves, 83
    Sambar Powder, 54
samosa. See Singara
samsara (repeated life cycles), 10
sattva (balance, goodness), 11, 293
sauces
    caramel sauce, 232–35
    cherry sauce, 232–35
    Sour Cream, for Beet Kofta,
      99–100
    Tomato Sauce with Saffron, 192
Savory Buttermilk Broth, 41
Savory Green Smoothie, 247
Savory Lassi, 249
sea salt, 283
seating arrangements, 17
semolina, wholegrain
    Semolina Crepes, 136
    Upma, 84
serving equipment, 288
shrikhand (strained yogurt), 211
Singara (savory pie), 150–53
slotted spoon, 288
soups
    Berry Soup, 224
    Carrot and Pumpkin Soup,
      124
sour cream
    basic recipe, 26
    Beet Kofta in Sour Cream
      Sauce, 99–100
    Sour Cream Dressing, 29
South Indian cuisine
    Eggplant Lentil Sambar with
      Curry Leaves, 83
    Ground Sweet Neem (Curry
      Leaf Powder), 50
    lemon rice, 71
    sambar, rasam masala, 53, 83
spelt flour ("spelt wheat"), benefits
  over wheat flour, 278
Spiced Green Beans, 88
Spiced Okra, 95
spice mixes. See also spices
    Chaat Masala, 61
    Curry Powder variations, 53
    Garam Masala, 58

Sambar Powder, 54
  storage, 54. See also specific mixes
Spice-Nut Paste, 41
spices. See also spice mixes
  adding to recipes, 260
  amchoor, 263
  anise, 263
  asafetida (hing), 263
  black peppercorn, 263
  cardamom (green), 263
  cautions using, 262
  cinnamon (cassia), 263–65
  cloves, 265
  coriander, 265
  curry leaves, 265
  fennel/fennel seeds, 265
  fenugreek, 266
  ginger, 266
  green chili, 266–67
  impact on appearance/texture of
    food, 260
  jeera (cumin), 267
  kala namak, 267
  kalonji (nigella seeds), 267
  licorice root, 267–68
  medicinal properties, 262
  mustard seeds (*rai)*, 268
  nutmeg, 268
  purchasing and storing, 260
  red chili peppers, 268
  saffron, 268–70
  star anise, 270
  as superfoods, 262
  tamarind, 270
  tej patta (Indian bay leaf), 271
  tempering, 260
  turmeric, 271
  whole, removing after cooking, 260
spinach
  blanching, 280
  Green Mung Dal with Fennel, 72
  as an ingredient, 280
  Palak Paneer (Spinach and Fresh
    Cheese), 112
  Pumpkin and Spinach Curry, 123
spoon, slotted, 288
star anise, 270
Stars and Atoms enterprise, 5–6
Steamed Vegetable Salad, 176

Steamed Yogurt Custard (Bhapa
  Doi), 200–201
stews (sambars), 83
stigmas (saffron), 268
storage. See also specific recipes
  butter, 22
  chenna, 42
  containers for, 288
  ghee, 25
  paneer, 43
  yogurt cheese, 37
strawberries
  Strawberry Halva, 208
  Strawberry Lassi, 248
sugar, 282–83
Summer Salad with Edible Flowers,
  167
Sunflower Seeds, Toasted, Watermelon Salad with, 168
Sweet Mango Yogurt (Amrakhand),
  211

T

Taittiriya Upanishad, 16, 294
takra (fermented milk drink)
  Sanskrit meaning, 38
  Savory Lassi, 249
  Takra (Churned Yogurt Drink),
    38
tamarind
  Date and Tamarind Chutney, 183
  as an ingredient, 270
  as a polishing agent, 270
tamas (ignorance), 293
Tartlets, Lemon and Caramel,
  222–23
Tea, Yogi, 252
tej patta (Indian bay leaf), 271
tempering
  Baby Potatoes in Yogurt-Tomato
    Sauce, 115
  Coconut Rice with Saffron, 68
  Eggplant Lentil Sambar with
    Curry Leaves, 83
  Green Mango Dal, 76
  Green Mung Dal with Fennel,
    72
  Jagannath Dal, 75
  Khandvi, 146–47

Kitchari (Rice and Dal Porridge), 79
Potato Curry from Mathura, 115
Quinoa Kitchari, 80
saucepans for, 284–85
Savory Buttermilk Broth, 41
Spiced Green Beans, 88
technique, 260
Upma, 84
tomatoes
Baby Potatoes in Yogurt-Tomato Sauce, 115
Green Bean Tomato Curry with Fried Cheese Balls, 111
as an ingredient, 282
Tomato Chutney, 191
Tomato Sauce with Saffron, 192
Tomato-Yogurt Sauce, 115
toor ("pigeon bean")
as an ingredient, 277
soaking before using, 76
toor dal, 277
toovar. See toor ("pigeon bean")
turmeric, 271

U
Upma (savory porridge), 84
urad, urad dal, 278

V
Vada (Lentil Doughnuts), 142
vaishnava celebration, 293
Vedic India
code of conduct, hospitality, 16
concept of life, 1–2
culture and literature, 294
esteem for cows in, 258
and the link between cooking and consciousness, 1–2
regional cuisines and meal planning, 15, 18
yogic etiquette, 17
vegetables, mixed
Bengali-Style Vegetables with Ground Mustard Seed, 126–27
Eggplant Lentil Sambar with Curry Leaves, 83
Kale and Cabbage Chips, 156
Roasted Vegetables, 120
Root Vegetable Frites, 107
Singara, 150–53
Steamed Vegetable Salad, 176
Upma, 84
vegetarian, pure, 10–11

W
Warm Apple Cider, 251
Watermelon Salad with Toasted Sunflower Seeds, 168
whey, 259
whole cane sugar, organic, 283
Wilted Green Salad, 171
woks, benefits of using, 284

Y
yellow mung
as an ingredient, 277
yellow mung dal, cooking time, 64

yoga cuisine
and *bhakti* tradition, 9
and cleanliness, 16–17
composing meals, 18–19
and conscious cooking, 1–2
and fulfillment, 9–10
and nonviolence (*ahimsa*), 2
practices associated with, 10
pure vegetarian, 10–11
sharing, as personal mission, 6–8
view of food in, 1
yellow mung dal, 277
yogic etiquette, 17
Yogi Tea, 252
yogurt
Amrakhand (Sweet Mango Yogurt), 211
Baby Potatoes in Yogurt-Tomato Sauce, 115
Banana Raita, 196
Bhapa Doi (Steamed Yogurt Custard), 200–201
Eggplant Raita, 197
Homemade Yogurt, 35
Savory Lassi, 249
strained (shrikhand), 211
Strawberry Lassi, 248
Takra (Churned Yogurt Drink), 38
Tomato-Yogurt Sauce, 115
Yogurt Cheese, 37
yogurt cheese
frying, tips, 155
for pakora, 155
Yogurt Cheese, 37
Yogurt Cheese Pakora, 155

ABOUT THE AUTHOR

Lakshmi Wennakoski-Bielicki grew up in the farthest nook of Scandinavia, Finland, but found her philosophical roots in ancient India when she took up the study and practice of bhakti-yoga (devotional service) in her early twenties. Although always interested in food as a medium for social interaction, she became fascinated by the spiritual value of cooking while living in a temple ashram for more than a decade in Greece and India. After moving back to Finland, Lakshmi ran the yoga studio Atma next to Helsinki University, where she offered vegetarian catering and cooking classes. She also wrote a cooking column in the Finnish yoga journal *Ananda*. In 2011 she started her blog, *Pure Vegetarian by Lakshmi*, which was nominated in 2012 by *Saveur* magazine as one of the best food blogs in the special-diets category. Her articles and recipes have been published in *Gourmet, Delicious,* and many other magazines and online publications. www.purevege.com